THE LANAHAN CASES

in

Developmental
Psychopathology

KAYLA F. BERNHEIM
is the author of

The LANAHAN Cases and Readings in Abnormal Behavior

Schizophrenia: Symptoms, Causes, and Treatments
(with Richard R. J. Lewine)

The Caring Family: Living with Chronic Mental Illness
(with Richard R. J. Lewine and Caroline T. Beale)

Working with Families of the Mentally Ill
(with Anthony F. Lehman)

LESLIE RESCORLA
is the editor of

Academic Instruction in Early Childhood:
Challenge or Pressure
(with Marion C. Hyson and Kathy Hirsh-Pasek)

LORRAINE ROCISSANO
is the author of

Helping Baby Talk

THE LANAHAN CASES

in

Developmental Psychopathology

—◄◎►—

Kayla F. Bernheim
Private Practice

Leslie Rescorla
Bryn Mawr College

Lorraine Rocissano
The Maryland School for the Blind

LANAHAN PUBLISHERS, INC.

Baltimore

The text of this book was composed in Sabon with display type set in Novarese.
Composition by Bytheway Publishing Services.
Manufacturing by Victor Graphics, Inc.

ISBN 0-9652687-5-6

LANAHAN PUBLISHERS, INC.
324 Hawthorne Road
Baltimore, MD 21210

1 2 3 4 5 6 7 8 9 0

CONTENTS

PART THREE Mood Disorders

PART FOUR Attention Deficit and Disruptive Behavior Disorders

PREFACE

This book of brief cases is designed to be used in courses in developmental psychopathology and child and adolescent abnormality. Case material gives students an opportunity to explore the richness of a person's experience over time in a way that discussions about diagnostic categories do not. While the core of any study of abnormal behavior is the individual case, most textbooks in this area, given the breadth of research and theory-building information they seek to cover, include little, if any, case material. When examples are offered, they are, of necessity, brief and fairly simplistic. We hope that the availability of more extensive exposure to individual cases will enrich students' ability to apply what they are learning, and expand the questions that they are able to generate.

The Cases

Each of the twenty-six cases in this volume is real. Identifying information has, of course, been changed to protect the privacy of the children and family, but they are otherwise true-to-life. Consequently, they are rarely simple and clear-cut. Instead, some illustrate how common it is for a youngster's symptoms to justify more than one diagnosis. Others reveal pitfalls in choosing or implementing therapeutic interventions. And while some of the children overcome their problems and go on to thrive, others are less fortunate. We believe that these "messy" cases, in addition to being more realistic, are more interesting. They will, we hope, inspire students to explore the issues about diagnostic practices, models of causation, choices of treatment, and possibilities for prevention of pathology.

Each of the cases is followed by three brief sections. The first, entitled "Thinking About The Case," examines how the symptoms described meet the diagnostic criteria under consideration and briefly summarizes current thinking about etiology, treatment, and prognosis. The second section, "The Developmental Perspective," takes up how the disorder is manifested at different developmental periods and how it evolves over time. We also look at how the particular developmental stage at which the illness began might affect the development of the disorder (for example, trigger it, ameliorate it, or exacerbate it) and how the disorder affects the accomplishment of normative developmental tasks. Finally, we include a list of "Questions to Consider" which we hope will stimulate students to think in a more creative way about what they have studied. These could be assigned by professors as paper topics or open-book essay questions.

Organization

The cases are organized and discussed in a manner that is generally consistent with the American Psychiatric Association's *Diagnostic and Statistical Manual*-IV, (*DSM*-IV). In addition to cases specified by *DSM*-IV as first occurring in infancy, childhood, or adolescence, we have included cases of common disorders whose onset can occur in childhood or adulthood, like mood, anxiety, and personality disorders. Because of space constraints, we have chosen not to include examples of all disorders of childhood (for instance, there are no mental retardation or sleep disorders), but rather have chosen those that are particularly common or vivid.

The introduction, "What is Developmental Psychopathology," lays out the perspective and assumptions of the developmental approach to psychopathology. Then, the seven parts of the book are organized in a loosely chronological way in terms of when the disorders first emerge. Therefore, Part One includes five cases illustrating syndromes that are generally agreed to have neurological foundations. Two are autistic spectrum disorders, one is a learning disability, one is fetal alcohol syndrome, and the last is a tic disorder. Part Two is comprised of six cases, five involving anxiety disorders and one illustrating somatoform disorder. Part Three on mood disorders and Four on attention deficit and disruptive behavior disorders follow *DSM*-IV rather closely, while Part Five looks at substance abuse and eating disorders, even drawing parallels between them. Part Six offers three examples of disturbed identity formation, drawn from disparate sections of *DSM-IV*. Finally, Part Seven compares and contrasts two examples of schizophrenia.

The Biopsychosocial Model

This volume has two philosophical premises. The first is laid out in the introduction: we believe that development and disorder affect each other throughout the lifespan. The second, which we have referred to as the biopsychosocial model, advances the hypothesis that disorders are almost always multiply-determined. Genetic, temperamental, and other constitutional factors interact with aspects of the home, peer, school, and community environment in complex ways. Both normal and abnormal development are a function of these interactions, rather than of the individual factors themselves. Thus, one youngster with a learning disability or anxiety is not the same as the next. Both biological and environmental factors will affect when and how disorders are manifest, as well as whether they have a good or bad outcome. Throughout, we have encouraged students to think about causation, course, treatment, and outcome in multifactoral ways.

One final note: Between us, we have over sixty years of clinical and academic experience. We continue to find our interactions with disturbed youngsters meaningful, our search for causes and treatments for disorders exciting, and our expectations for the future hopeful. We hope that students will approach these cases with the deep sense of respect and curiosity that these youngsters and families have engendered in us.

Kayla F. Bernheim
Leslie Rescorla
Lorraine Rocissano

November, 1998

WHAT IS DEVELOPMENTAL
PSYCHOPATHOLOGY?

———◄○►———

Two-year-old Amy does not seem to communicate well. In fact, she seems isolated in a world of her own. Five-year-old Matthew is incapacitated by the fear that he or someone close to him is going to die. Anne is impulsive and disorganized, she drives her parents and teachers crazy with her oppositional behavior, and she gets into trouble with her friends. Caitlin, an adolescent, is seriously depressed and clearly abusing alcohol and cocaine. Ben is a twelve-year-old who touches the corners of things hundreds of times a day and holds his breath whenever he sees something "bad." Barbara, age twelve, was sent to the hospital when she ate nothing for five days after already having lost many pounds on a three-month crash diet.

Twenty-five years ago, we would have had few diagnoses to use for these children and we would have known very little about how common or unusual their symptoms were, whether they were likely to recover, or how we might best treat their problems. Today, however, we take an approach to children called *developmental psychopathology*.

In 1984, Alan Sroufe and Michael Rutter defined developmental psychopathology as "the study of the origins and course of individual patterns of behavioral manifestation, whatever the age of onset, whatever the causes, whatever the transformations in behavioral manifestation, and however complex the course of the developmental pattern may be." This definition is complicated, and we will spend several pages breaking it down and examining each of its elements. But first we will make a few general points.

Researchers and clinicians taking a developmental approach to psychopathology seek to understand how and why individuals become maladjusted or disordered by studying maladaptive functioning as it develops over time. Hence, developmental psychopathology is an approach to disorders that is closely linked to developmental psychology. We look at normative development as the baseline against which maladaptive behaviors are evaluated. It is when youngsters fail to accomplish the "tasks" associated with various developmental stages, or when they do not show the expected age-related changes in areas such as language, interpersonal relations, behavioral self-control, morality, and emotional regulation, that we suspect the presence of some form of psychopathology. At the same time, developmental psychopathology is also tightly linked to abnormal psychology because we can best understand clinical conditions by examining their development over time. So when we try to understand the nature of a current disorder, to choose an appropriate treatment, and to make reasonable predictions about outcome, we now seek to know what precursors of the disorder were apparent earlier in a person's life, how previous life events predisposed the individual toward developing the disorder, and how well the person functioned in different areas of his or her life before becoming mentally ill.

The central role developmental psychopathology plays as a perspective integrating developmental and abnormal psychology—traditionally, two separate domains of inquiry—is evident in two major trends of the past twenty-five years. First, non-clinical developmental psychology researchers have turned increasingly to the study of individual differences in adaptive functioning. Second, researchers in abnormal psychology are finding it more and more illuminating to study the developmental pathways by which various adult disorders develop.

Empirical Data Base

The definition that Alan Sroufe and Michael Rutter proposed contains many of the key elements of the developmental psychopathology perspective. First, the word "study" reflects the fact that developmental psychopathology is a field with a strong and ever-increasing empirical data base. Much of this research is both epidemiological and longitudinal in nature. That is, researchers study large samples of children, some well adjusted and others less so, and then follow these children over long periods of time, enabling researchers to trace the developing course of both adaptive functioning and maladaptation.

Life-Span Orientation

The words "origins" and "course" in the definition indicate that developmental psychopathology has a strong historical or life-span orientation. Researchers using this perspective look for constitutional vulnerabilities that may put children at risk for later maladjustment or temperamental assets that may serve as "protective" factors helping children to emerge relatively unscathed from later negative life experiences. For example, a highly reactive, anxious, or irritable child may be more at risk for disorder than an adaptable, calm, or optimistic child. Similarly, social experiences in a child's development either can be risk factors for later maladaptation or can serve to buffer the child against future environmental stressors. So, a child who suffers early neglect and abuse by a mentally ill parent might well be at risk for later maladjustment, but that child's close relationship with a nurturing grandmother could serve as protection from severe psychopathology. Developmental psychopathologists try to find links between past and present, such as by looking at "subclinical precursors" of later disorders. Why do some noncompliant and aggressive toddlers grow up to be violent adolescent criminals, but most do not? Developmental psychopathologists also look at how a particular disorder changes with age and development. For example, they seek to understand how a highly anxious girl who manifests severe separation problems as a preschooler becomes excessively fearful as a school-age child, is unable to sleep away from home as an adolescent, and develops agoraphobia as a young woman.

Developmental psychopathologists also examine how maladaptation interferes with the accomplishment of normative developmental tasks. For example, the anxious preschooler with a separation problem may try to avoid going to school, cry excessively when she gets there, sit in her cubby with her blanket, and spend a lot of time on her teacher's lap. All of these behaviors interfere with her learning the social skills of give-and-take necessary for negotiating peer interaction. In effect, she will not master new challenges in the classroom or on the playground, which could make her feel even more unhappy and thereby increase her avoidant behavior.

Patterns of Adaptive and Maladaptive Behavior

Central to the developmental psychopathology approach is the study of "individual patterns of behavioral maladaptation." Researchers in this field look at individual differences, at how a given child falls on polar dimensions such as introversion versus extroversion, optimism versus pessimism, impulsivity versus reflectivity, and emotional explosivity versus self-control. Furthermore, they search for patterns and configurations, that is, systematic regularities in how groups of symptoms cluster together. For instance, many children who are impulsive tend to be highly distractible, overly active, forgetful, inattentive, and reckless. Children with this set of problems are also likely to be aggressive and oppositional. Researchers use statistical procedures to discover patterns of co-occurring symptoms, and they derive characteristic profiles of maladjustment. Once these patterns are reliably established, they may be included as diagnostic categories in revisions of the *Diagnostic and Statistical Manual*, now in its fourth edition (*DSM*-IV). Psychiatrists and psychologists use the *DSM* to classify the various types of psychopathologies.

The term "behavioral maladaptation" highlights the strong adaptive functioning orientation that is characteristic of this field. Children who have psychological disorders often fail to acquire the skills normally developing children master, and consequently they have difficulty meeting the normative demands of their developmental period. For example, autistic children fail to acquire normal language, play, and social interaction skills. They also manifest numerous deviant symptoms characteristic of the disorder, such as echolalic speech, repetitive and stereotypic behavior, and gaze aversion. Depressed children might fail to learn the social skills needed to deal with peers.

Onset and Course of Disorders

As Sroufe and Rutter's definition implies, the developmental psychopathology perspective recognizes that "age of onset" is an important focus of study. Some disorders, such as autism and attention-deficit hyperactivity disorder, are known to be of early onset and to continue throughout life. On the other hand, the behaviors characteristic of many disorders may change over time, and there is wide variation across individuals in the degree of improvement or remission that occurs with age. For example, the attention-deficit hyperactivity disorder symptom of impulsivity may manifest itself as running into the street in a preschooler but as having auto accidents and poor judgment about drinking alcohol in an adolescent; an adult may manifest impulsivity by changing residences or jobs more frequently than most other people. In some disorders, age of onset can be an important predictor of later outcome. For example, children who display serious conduct problems (e.g., aggression, rule violation, destructiveness, deceit, belligerence) before the age of eleven or twelve may be more likely to become criminal adults than individuals who first manifest such symptoms as adolescents.

Multiple Causes and Changing Symptoms

A central tenet of the developmental psychopathology perspective is that there are multiple factors that contribute to either adaptive or maladaptive functioning. Thus, when Sroufe and Rutter say "whatever the causes," they allude to the multiple etiologies or causes that the developmental psychopathology researcher must take into account in trying to understand how maladjustment develops, or why some children at risk turn out so well. Many different factors must all be taken into account in trying to understand how adaptation or maladaptation is constructed over time. These include characteristics inherent in the individual (e.g., level of intelligence, physical attractiveness, temperamental factors, biological vulnerabilities); family factors (e.g., psychopathology in parents, marital issues, socioeconomic status, child-rearing style); school factors (e.g., handling of learning or behavioral difficulties, teachers' attitudes and behaviors); and sociocultural factors (e.g., peer group influences, discrimination, disadvantaged neighborhoods).

One of the reasons this field is challenging is that the same basic disorder can manifest itself differently at different points in development. Sroufe and Rutter refer to this when they mention "transformations in behavioral manifestation." Depression is a good example of a disorder that can emerge at various points in development but that may manifest itself differently at different ages. For example, younger depressed children show less guilt and hopelessness than do school-age children, whereas adolescents show more co-morbid conduct disorder and substance abuse problems and are more likely to be suicidal than either preschoolers or school-age children. We also know that the same stressful life event can have different impacts, depending on the age, gender, and previous experience of the child. For example, research has shown that divorce has a more negative impact on boys than on girls, but that a mother's remarriage tends to be more problematic for girls than for boys.

Positive Pathways/Deviant Pathways

Finally, Sroufe and Rutter refer to the complexity that is characteristic of the "developmental pattern." Developmental psychopathologists often use the term "pathway." This is because they see development as proceeding along a course, with the "straight" and positive pathways being that of developmental adaptation and the deviations from those pathways being various forms of developmental maladaptation. This metaphor of a pathway suggests that there are forks in the road, places where a youngster may make a choice to deviate from the pathway of adaptation; the farther the child gets down this deviant pathway, the harder it is to return to the path of adaptation. This can be seen clearly in youngsters who begin engaging in antisocial behavior in grade school, come to be regarded as "bad kids," and soon find that the only children who will be their friends are other deviant children, who lead them further down the path of delinquency.

Although it is generally the case that the farther one travels down a deviant pathway the harder it is to return to the path of adaptation, this is not always the case. Even if a child travels far down a deviant path, there are often routes back to the main pathway, actions that can be taken to help a child return to the developmental trajectory of healthy adaptation. This can often occur in periods of major developmental transition. A girl who has spent her adolescence struggling with an eating disorder may come to a point of realizing, as she is facing high school graduation, that life is passing her by and that she must conquer these problems, become independent of her family, and move on to the developmental tasks of young adulthood. Sometimes an insight or a conviction such as this at an important developmental turning point can be a crucial first step in a young person's journey back to the pathway of adaptive functioning.

From the perspective of developmental psychopathology, continuity is a major truth, but so is change. Thus, on average, children who have had healthy adaptation in the earlier years of their lives are likely to weather adolescence without major maladjustment. Similarly, children whose early years have been marked by serious maladaptation are, in general, at risk for continuing psychopathology. On the other hand, there are many cases of well-adjusted school-age children who develop significant psychopathology before they complete the adolescent years, and there are many other cases of youngsters who have been significantly disturbed in an earlier developmental period and then seem to recover and thereafter have minimal adjustment problems in later life.

As you read through the cases in this book, you will meet many young people. They vary in age, gender, socioeconomic background, intelligence, personality, and adaptive competencies, but what they have in common is that their development is marked by maladaptation. The children and adolescents whose stories are told here illustrate a full range of problems that are seen in clinics treating young people. Some have disorders that are relatively mild, whereas others are severely disturbed. Many of these types of psychopathologies are very common, whereas others are relatively rare. For many of the troubled children here, the right combination of help provided by professionals and support provided by others in the children's lives, coupled with a determination to change on the part of each child, led to treatment success and a good resolution of the presenting problems.

Unfortunately, not all of the youngsters whose histories you will be reading were so lucky. Whether because of the inherent intractability of their disorders, the lack of knowledge about how best to help, the limits in skill of the therapists, the impediments to treatment compliance in families, or the ultimate resistance to change in the children, these youngsters could not be guided back to the pathway of healthy adaptation, at least not during the time period of their lives described here. However, as you read through the stories in this book, keep in mind the wisdom of the great English novelist George Eliot, who captured the essence of the developmental psychopathology perspective more than one hundred years before it became a field of psychological study: "For the fragment of a life, however typical, is not the sample of an even web; promises may not be kept, and an ardent outset may be followed by declension; latent powers may find a long-awaited opportunity; a past error may urge a grand retrieval."

Reference

Sroufe, A., & Rutter, M. (1984) The domain of developmental psychopathology. *Child Development*, 55, 17–29.

PART ONE

Developmental, Learning, and Psychoneurological Disorders

———◀o▶———

S ome youngsters are born with neurological or other organic conditions that impair their cognitive, language, motor, or social development. While the causes of these disorders are presumed to be primarily physical, they have wide-ranging psychological and social consequences for the affected children and their families. The *DSM*-IV lists the following as developmental disorders (which are coded on Axis II): mental retardation, specific learning disorders, motor skills disorders, communication disorders, and pervasive developmental disorders.

In this section, we begin with two cases of pervasive developmental disorder, which, as its name suggests, involves deficits in virtually all areas of functioning from academic to interpersonal. Amy, afflicted with autism, experiences profound deficits and is likely to become a severely disabled adult, whereas Seth's symptoms are milder and less impairing. We hope that reading both of these cases will give you a sense of the range of functioning involved in pervasive developmental disorders. We have included a case of dyslexia, a relatively common reading disability, as an example of the specific learning disorders.

We have also included two cases of nondevelopmental disorders. There is no specific *DSM*-IV category for fetal alcohol syndrome (FAS). Instead, a youngster with FAS would be diagnosed with each of the specific intellectual or behavioral problems exhibited. We have elected to include an FAS case in this section because the neurological impairment caused by exposing the fetal brain to alcohol is, like that of the developmental disorders, lifelong and pervasive and can be severely debilitating.

Finally, *DSM*-IV lists tic disorders, of which Tourette's is the classic example, under their own category. We have included a Tourette's case in this section because it is generally agreed that Tourette's has a neurological basis. Further, like the other disorders in this section, it emerges relatively early in life and has a chronic course if left untreated.

1

AUTISTIC DISORDER:
THE CASE OF AMY F

AT TWO YEARS OLD, Amy was not yet talking, and her parents were beginning to worry. She had started with a few words at thirteen months, right on time, but had stopped soon after. When Amy was almost three, Mr. and Mrs. F brought their daughter, a beautiful, curly-mopped little girl, to a friend, a psychologist who studied language development, for an informal evaluation.

The family history was unremarkable. Amy's parents were a young married couple, who doted on their only child. Mr. F was a physics professor at a local university who, although deeply engaged in his research and in the struggle to achieve tenure, played with and read to his daughter each evening. His wife, although college educated, had elected to stay at home until Amy reached school age. They seemed a warm and engaging couple. There had been no history of mental illness on either side of their family, nor had there been any complications of pregnancy or birth. Amy had breezed through the early developmental milestones—holding her head up, rolling over, sitting, standing, walking—at an average or quicker than average pace.

The psychologist videotaped a play session with Amy and her mother, and in reviewing it, this is what she saw: Amy was a child who was fascinated with things but virtually uninterested in people.

Amy's way of playing with toys was decidedly odd. She would pick up a toy, examine it visually and with her hands, then throw it down and pick up another. Her play was manipulative, rather than symbolic. That is, she never used the toys to create a pretend scenario, as most children do. In fact, she didn't seem to understand what toys were for; she was interested only in their shapes, colors, and textures.

During the play session, Amy's mom sat or laid on the floor with Amy, talking to her and trying to engage her. Not only did Amy not speak, but she acted as if her mother were not there. She never looked at her, nor did she respond to her mother's questions, comments, and suggestions. It was clear that she could hear, because she noticed noises in the hall and music coming from a radio in the next room. She simply did not respond to any language input.

The psychologist was struck by one other curious phenomenon. At one point in the session, Amy was drawn to the hallway by a noise. Arriving at the doorway, she stared, rapt, down the hall for four or five long minutes. The hallway was empty of people and objects. All the psychologist could see was the pattern made by the lights on the ceiling: light, dark, light, dark. When she mentioned her observation to Amy's mom, Mrs. F related that Amy often stood, entranced in the same way, in front of a poster she had in her room at home. Trying to shift her attention would generally result in a tantrum. She herself could never understand Amy's particular fascination with this poster, but, interestingly enough, it, too, had alternating blocks of darkness and light.

Amy's parents had not really thought of her behavior as disturbed. They attributed her lack of interaction to her lack of speech. They assumed that, once she learned to talk, everything would be fine. In the meantime, they treated her like a normal child.

The psychologist suggested to Amy's parents that the problem might be more pervasive than they thought and that a psychiatric consultation might be of use. With some trepidation, they accepted a referral to a child psychiatrist, who diagnosed Amy as having childhood schizophrenia. He told the dismayed parents that something traumatic must have happened to Amy to induce her profound emotional separation from others and urged them to search their memories for situations that might qualify. The only thing they could come up with was that Mrs. F had gone away overnight to visit her parents when Amy was eight months old. The psychiatrist felt that this separation from her major attachment figure might indeed have been so awful for Amy that she developed the isolation as a psychological defense against any future loss of a love object. He further implied that perhaps Mrs. F's choice to leave Amy overnight at such a "sensitive" age was an indication of a more general lack of sensitivity to the nurturance needs of her child.

Mrs. F was devastated by the psychiatrist's pronouncement. She had never meant to hurt her child, but here was an expert saying that she was responsible for inflicting serious, possibly permanent, damage on Amy's psyche. Mr. F had a host of conflicting feelings. He loved his wife and he felt protective of her. He wanted to support her, but, on the other hand, if she had damaged his daughter, he couldn't help but be furious.

Mr. and Mrs. F continued to see the psychiatrist for several more sessions, but at the same time they began to read all that they could find about childhood schizophrenia. In their reading, they stumbled across an article about childhood autism that seemed to describe Amy's behavior perfectly. They were particularly struck by the description of how autistic children require ritualistic sameness in their environment. Amy listened to the same piece of music hundreds and hundreds of times. She would eat only a small number of foods, prepared in only one way. At the moment, she was keen on bologna sandwiches on white bread with the edges cut off, mayonnaise only on one side, the sandwich cut crosswise into quarters. If any step was missing or wrong, she pitched an enormous fit, throwing herself around and screaming until another sandwich was made exactly as she wanted it.

They were also struck by the article's description of "autistic aloneness." Amy seemed to fit it exactly: She seemed totally walled in. She existed in a world of things where no one else was invited. She didn't dislike people; she simply ignored them. She wouldn't sit on her mother's lap or cuddle. She didn't follow her parents around, even with her eyes.

Mr. and Mrs. F decided to seek a second opinion regarding Amy's diagnosis and treatment. They took her to a program for autistic children where a multidisciplinary evaluation by a psychiatrist, a psychologist, a speech pathologist, and an occupational therapist confirmed the diagnosis of autism.

Some treatment programs for autistic children follow a strictly behavioral model in which youngsters are rewarded (e.g., with candy) for behavior that brings them into contact with others. First eye contact is rewarded, then touching and speaking. The goal is to gradually shape interactional behaviors. At the same time, autistic behaviors, like tantrums or self-mutilative behavior, might be punished. Since autistic children are not innately rewarded by social contact, "time out," which usually works well for normal children, cannot be used with them.

The program in which Amy was enrolled uses a combination of one-to-one teaching of developmentally appropriate academic and functional skills along with individual work sessions that are structured in such a way that the child can complete work tasks independently. At first, Amy could do only very simple sorting tasks that took less than a minute to complete. But over time she became able to read a list of relatively detailed task instructions and attend to her work for extended periods. The program, called TEACCH (Treatment and Education of Autistic and related Communication Handicapped Children), focuses on "learning how to learn." Because autistic children generally have stronger visual/spatial skills than verbal skills, the TEACCH program includes many visual cues about task expectations, schedules, and transitions as a way to reduce confusion and anxiety while helping children acquire new skills. Amy's parents are hopeful that she might improve, but they know that they must wait and see. In the meantime, they are learning all they can about autism. They have joined a support group composed of other parents of autistic children. Here they can grieve the loss of the person that Amy might have become and gain strength to accept the person that she is.

Thinking about the Case

Autism is one of several pervasive developmental disorders in which impairments in social development and communication skills are prominent. It is called a "pervasive" disorder because of the devastating impact on overall developmental progression. Motor behavior, information processing and other intellectual abilities, language development, and social learning are all affected. Hypersensitivities in one or more of the senses are also common. Autism is about as common as deafness, occurring in approximately 4 out of every 10,000 children. Amy's case is fairly typical: delayed receptive and expressive language, lack of relatedness with others, and ritualistic and stereotypical behavior patterns.

A few individuals with autism (called "autistic savants") display marked intelligence, even brilliance in certain areas. For example, some can replicate on the piano any musical piece, no matter how complicated, having heard it only once. Yet they are unable to play even the simplest melody from written music or to compose even the most elementary tune. Others are numbers whizzes. They are able to perform instant calculations of very large numbers. Yet these same people often cannot make change at the grocery store. Some have amassed huge amounts of knowledge about a small area of information. For example, one child could recite all of the bus routes across the country. By now you have guessed the rest: This same youngster was unable to find his way to the corner store and back home.

The cause or causes of autism are not yet known. The hypothesis put forth by the first psychiatrist who evaluated Amy was common at one time. Parents of autistic children were once thought to be cold, aloof, and unable to create a warm connection with their children. However, the fact that most autistic children have perfectly normal siblings made such a hypothesis unlikely to be true, and, in fact, research efforts have been unable to demonstrate any patterns of parental behavior or characteristics that are related to autism. Since not all mental health professionals are equally conversant with the latest research in every area, parents would be well advised to seek a second opinion as well as to do some research on their own, like Amy's parents did.

Researchers today are looking more at possible biological underpinnings and are finding some things: First, autistic individuals have higher rates of abnormal brain wave patterns than do non-autistic controls. Second, a variety of other functional and structural differences in the brain exist between autistic and non-autistic individuals. Third, there is a higher than expected incidence of seizure disorder as autistic youngsters reach adulthood. Further, obstetrical and perinatal complications are found more often in the history of autistic individuals than in controls. Twin studies indicate a possible genetic link as well, although the vulnerability appears to exist for a variety of cognitive impairments, rather than for autism alone.

Even with these findings, the prognosis for autism is still quite poor. Over half of the children diagnosed with autism are unable to function as independent adults. Children who receive intensive treatment and whose educational programs are modified to meet their unique learning needs appear to make progress. For a very few individuals, improvement can be dramatic, with autistic symptoms diminishing markedly. For others, especially those with mental retardation, progress is limited. Nonetheless, the prognosis for most children diagnosed with autism in this decade is far better than it was thirty years ago, when very little was known about the disorder or how to treat it. For all autistic children, treatment that begins before the age of two is associated with better outcomes. Still, fewer than 5 percent of individuals with childhood autism are indistinguishable from "normal" individuals at adulthood.

The Developmental Perspective

It is likely that the development of autistic youngsters is disrupted as the fetus develops. Once the youngster is born, abnormalities appear quite early. Autistic infants, like Amy, show abnormal indifference to their parents and may even attempt to avoid being touched or cuddled. Many are hypersensitive to stimuli of all kinds: Rain on the roof startles and panics them; they cannot adapt to new foods; the texture of their clothes is unbearable.

Most crucial, perhaps, is the lack of development of language. Many will not speak at all, others will have delayed and bizarre speech, and others may begin to speak normally but then stop after a brief time as Amy did. Unlike deaf children, whose language does not develop because they do not hear, but who are capable of normal communication in another medium, autistic youngsters do not communicate normally in nonverbal ways. That is, they don't use facial expression, gesture, and sounds to convey meaning and don't seem to understand these communicative cues when provided by others. If this capacity for communication does not develop adequately, intellectual and social development cannot proceed normally. It is not surprising, then, that autistic individuals who develop language have a much better prognosis than those who do not.

Even for autistic individuals, development brings changes. Adults with autism tend to be somewhat less difficult to manage, although no less strange. The frequency of tantrums decreases, as practiced patterns of behavior and years of experience appear to allow some sense to be made of the world. Socialization of some sort, although still highly abnormal, increases over time as well.

Questions to Consider

1. Because symptoms of different disorders can overlap, misdiagnoses, like the one given to Mr. and Mrs. F, are not as uncommon as one might wish. How might a parent with a disturbed child protect against this possibility?

2. If you were the parent of an autistic child, what information would you want in order to decide which treatment program to place your child in? How would you go about getting this information?

3. What effect might the presence of an autistic child have on the life of a family? How might it affect the parents' relationship? How might it affect the siblings as they face their own developmental tasks? How might it affect the relationship between the parents and the well siblings?

4. What are some reasons that early intervention might be important in the treatment of autism?

5. Assume, for the moment, that some specific brain abnormality will be found in persons with autism. Would you still consider it a psychological disorder? Why or why not?

2

HIGH-FUNCTIONING PERVASIVE
DEVELOPMENTAL DISORDER:
THE CASE OF SETH B

TEN-YEAR-OLD Seth came from an accomplished family. His mother was a violinist in the symphony orchestra of their mid-sized city, and his father was a successful self-employed architect. For a time, it seemed that Seth would follow in his parents' footsteps—at least until he entered school.

As an infant and toddler, Seth had presented no problem to his parents. Early on he could play for hours by himself and, by the age of two, he was reciting television commercials by rote memory even though his communication to other people was odd and "off base," even for a young child. At three, he developed a fascination with knots. He took to carrying around a piece of rope, practicing over and over the nautical knots that his father had taught him during their summer sailing trips. He played, ate, and slept with his rope. It was in his hand or looped around his waist at all times.

Thus, it was a shock to his parents when Seth was thrown out of the private nursery school they had carefully chosen. The headmaster described Seth as unmanageable. Apparently, he was unable to get along with the other children. What's more, he'd strike out at them with little if any provocation. Attempts by his teacher to contain or redirect him met with even greater storms of rage. When he kicked her as hard as he could in the shin, it was the last straw. Mrs. B felt that Seth had been made a scapegoat. While she admitted that her son could be irritable and bossy, she had never seen any signs of rage around the house. She was glad to have him out of there, because she thought that the school environment must have been much too rigid for him.

Unfortunately, Seth's behavioral problems continued when he entered the excellent public primary school in his neighborhood. He didn't seem to have any particular learning difficulty, but he was described by his teachers in both kindergarten and first grade as impulsive, aggressive, and inattentive.

Toward the middle of first grade, Seth's pediatrician offered a tentative diagnosis of "attention-deficit hyperactivity disorder" and prescribed stimulant medication, which had been shown to be effective in calming and focusing hyperactive youngsters. With the medication, Seth seemed a bit better able to stay in his seat and on task in school, but his interpersonal problems continued. He was virtually friendless.

Seth seemed not to care, though, since his growing fascination with knots was a solitary pursuit. By this time, he was beginning to draw elaborate pictures of knots, beautifully shaded. The art teacher said the drawings were very advanced for a youngster of his age. But Seth's preoccupation with knots was apparently part of the problem with peers. His teacher reported that his conversation was almost wholly about knots. His idea of a good time was to get other children to watch him make an elaborate knot, and he seemed to have no idea that this might bore them to tears. In fact, he wasn't able to understand what others might be thinking or feeling in any situation. He appeared totally self-centered.

By third grade, even Seth's parents had to admit that he was strange. His conversation was idiosyncratic and awkward. He seemed not to understand what to say when he had to interact with others. He'd repeat sentences over and over despite being assured that he was understood. He had no interest in playing with other children. Left to himself, he seemed perfectly content, but interfered with he was a terror. Seth's parents decided to get a full educational and psychological evaluation from the developmental unit of the local hospital. There, intelligence testing revealed an interesting pattern of scores: While his eye-hand coordination and vocabulary were good, Seth's comprehension of the world around him and his social judgment were remarkably poor. Interestingly, while he could remember how to draw a complicated knot he had seen only once, he could not remember a sequence of four numbers for even a few seconds. Further observation of Seth's behavior and careful evaluation of data provided by his teachers and parents contributed to the final diagnosis: pervasive developmental disorder of the Asperger's type.

Seth's parents experienced a combination of horror, disbelief, and relief. Such a disorder implied lifelong difficulties in virtually all domains of living. How could such a thing be true of their clearly bright and talented child? On the other hand, the confusing range of behaviors that Seth exhibited now made sense—they had a name. Seth's parents put into action their own formidable intellectual and emotional skills. They began to read all they could about autism and Asperger's syndrome. They learned that Asperger's syndrome is the term used in recent years for children on the pervasive developmental disorder or autistic spectrum who have normal I.Q. and good language skills and whose social deficits, restricted interests, and stereotyped behavior are less bizarre than in "classic" autism. Seth's parents decided to try to help their son achieve whatever he could by enrolling him in a special school for autistic children. There, for the first time, he didn't stand out like a dandelion in a manicured lawn. For the first time, he wasn't singled out for criticism by teachers or other kids. Seth's tantrums decreased within the first few weeks due to the staff's understanding of his need for predictability of routine and his resistance to any external demand that he move from one activity to another. Frequent breaks were a part of the program, and the expectation for sustained attention was decreased.

Further, the staff at the school creatively capitalized on Seth's love of knots. Virtually all of his papers at school were about knots: poems about knots, essays about knots, research papers about the various uses of knots in people's work lives, sports, and crafts. In ninth grade, he even won a citywide educational achievement award for creating a video game in which participants untied increasingly complicated knots rather than splattering increasingly powerful enemies.

The school also provided specialized training in social skills. Role-playing exercises taught students simple responses to various social situations that they then memorized by rote repetition. Thus they learned how to order in a restaurant, how to ask politely when they needed something, how to respond if someone inadvertently hurt or frustrated them. A token economy system, in which socially appropriate behaviors were rewarded with tokens that could be exchanged for trinkets or foods, also helped shape students' social behavior.

Seth was among the most high-functioning students in his school. Throughout ninth grade, he had campaigned with his parents to allow him to attend public school. Apparently, he was not so indifferent to others that he was unaware of the stigma associated with attending his school. His teachers felt that they had taught him everything they could and that he might benefit from contact with nondisabled adolescents. His parents, while worried that he would again be targetted and shunned, agreed that he needed preparation for entry into the "real world." Mutual strategizing among Seth's parents, his current teachers, and the special education committee of the public high school produced a plan in which Seth would be in a small, self-contained classroom with other students who had learning difficulties. He would be "mainstreamed" for gym, music, art, and computer programming. If he did well, additional mainstreaming could gradually be added over the next two years. His parents hoped that by senior year Seth would be ready to enter college, where he might make some kind of an independent life for himself. It remains to be seen whether that hope will be justified.

Thinking about the Case

Compared with Amy (Case 1), Seth's prognosis is quite good.While he shows many of the symptoms of autism, including bizarre language, intellectual deficits with islands of strength, and impaired social development, his overall ability to function is significantly higher. Together these cases illustrate that pervasive developmental disability is a continuum rather than a discrete "you have it or you don't" diagnosis.

Students like Seth often slip through the cracks in the educational system. Because their disability is difficult to diagnose, they may go without appropriate services for years. They may be mislabeled as having attention-deficit disorder, as Seth was, or as having oppositional disorder, obsessive-compulsive disorder, or some other problem entirely. Once they are correctly identified, there may not be a program appropriate for them. It was lucky that Seth settled into the school for autistic youngsters, despite the fact that he functioned at a higher level than most of them. Had he not, it is unlikely that the public school would have been able to develop a program specifically suited to his needs.

We do not know why some people are severely disabled, like Amy, and why some, like Seth, are more mildly affected. It is likely that there are multiple biological causes of pervasive developmental disorder, each leading to a different subtype with a different constellation of symptoms and a different prognosis.

The Developmental Perspective

While Amy's autism may effectively halt her intellectual and social development, Seth's disability alters the course of his. She may never be able to pick out the repetitive patterns of language and will thus be shut out of the world. Seth, on the other hand, has enough ability to communicate with and understand others to manage some sense of connection. While she may be in a closely supervised setting, perhaps even some sort of institution, all of her life, Seth looks forward to creating some sort of life in society. Thus, each developmental milestone will present major challenges. How, for example, does a youngster with Seth's social awkwardness and impaired judgment manage the emotional and social complexities of adolescence? How will he make the transition to independent functioning required of young adults? At each of these stages, his cognitive and emotional deficits will impede learning from his experiences, so that his progress can be expected to be delayed at best. Further, it is likely that some skill areas will continue to be more developed than others, resulting in an inconsistent pattern of adult functioning. For example, he may have greater success holding a job with low demands for social interaction, such as accounting, than establishing an intimate relationship with another person.

Questions to Consider

1. What were the pros and cons of sending Seth to a special school? What do you think are the prospects for his success in reentering public school? Why?

2. What sorts of jobs or professions might Seth be able to succeed in? What problems do you anticipate that he would have in a work setting as an adult? What kinds of special supports might he need?

3. What are some ways to test the hypothesis that there are several different, discrete disorders lumped together under the heading "pervasive developmental disability" rather than a unitary continuum in which symptoms range from mild to severe?

3

DYSLEXIA: THE CASE OF NED L

TWELVE-YEAR-OLD Ned L reluctantly followed the principal down the hall to the counselor's office. He shuffled his feet and hung his head. His cheeks were flaming red. He had gotten into trouble with his fifth-grade teacher for the third time that day—and for the umpteenth time that week. And it was only the first week of November.

"We're at the end of our rope with him," the principal angrily told the counselor. Giving Ned a stern look, she recited a lengthy list of misdeeds, everything from breaking his neighbor's pencil to using foul language. "But the worst of it is his attitude," she reported. "He acts as though his teacher has no right to ask him to do anything. He wants to sit with his feet up and his head in the clouds. He seems to think that schoolwork is too far beneath him to be bothered with! When I asked him why he was behaving this way, all he would say was 'I dunno.' Maybe you can get him to make some sense." With that, she stormed off down the hall.

As the counselor questioned Ned about school—what subjects he liked or didn't like, what he did for fun, if he felt comfortable socially—he became increasingly quiet, giving only evasive answers like "I don't know" or "I guess" as he squirmed in his chair. Finally, with a look that spoke volumes about his feelings of anger and resentment, he blurted, "School is just stupid! I hate everything about it and I don't care if they throw me out!"

The counselor called a meeting of Ned's teachers along with his mother, a library aide, and his father, a worker with the city sanitation department. All agreed that Ned had always been a quiet, even shy child who until recently had tried to melt into the woodwork. Then over the course of fourth grade he had become increasingly sullen and uncooperative, refusing to do his chores or join in family activities at home and becoming belligerent and oppositional at school. In both contexts, he seemed always to be involved in fighting with his peers.

Teachers, counselor, and parents alike were baffled by these changes in Ned. Some thought that he was being influenced by some older boys in the neighborhood who always seemed to be in trouble themselves. Others wondered if his irritability and lack of cooperation might reflect an underlying depression. Ned's mother expressed concern that having two working parents might have left Ned feeling neglected.

The guidance counselor suggested that Ned be placed on a behavioral program at school and at home, where evidence of good behavior would be rewarded with certain privileges or treats that Ned desired. For a time, the behavioral program seemed to be working. At least he no longer picked fights or talked back to his teachers. He did his chores. But after several weeks it became apparent that his underlying attitude had not really improved. He was willing to control his behavior enough to earn the rewards, but he still resisted putting any effort into his schoolwork. At home, he seemed glued to the television. At this point Ned's counselor felt that further consultation with a child psychologist was in order and referred the parents to a well-respected professional in their area.

The history that Ned's parents gave to the child psychologist indicated that Ned, the third child in his family, was the product of a healthy, full-term pregnancy. His development had proceeded normally during the early childhood years, although he had been late to talk. He had not started really talking until well past his third birthday, and even at age four, his sentences were much simpler than those of his peers. In addition, his speech had been hard to understand, and he had had a small vocabulary. His mother felt that he had always been a more sensitive and vulnerable child than either of her other children. As a result, he was both closer to and more dependent on her than were his siblings.

Kindergarten, a half-day program, had gone well for Ned. But he had had difficulty with reading in the first grade. Since he had a fall birthday, he was a bit younger than some of the other children, and his teacher felt that an extra year in the first grade would give him time to mature both cognitively and socially.

Ned seemed happy enough in both years of first grade. He brought home good grades in math, but his report card always showed that his reading wasn't as strong as it could be. Teachers gave him poor marks for effort, saying that he didn't seem to be working on reading at all. They suggested that his parents be sure to read to him and have him read to them for a little while each night. Mrs. L said she felt guilty that they had never really done this. Second through fourth grades had been more of the same. In retrospect, Ned's parents felt that he had been unhappy at school for some time. His grades had been consistently marginal, which they could understand since he resisted doing any homework. During the weeks that school was in session, he seemed tense and easily "set off," except on weekends, when he woke up early and was ready for fun.

Mr. L stated that he was angry at the school for not doing more to help Ned, who he felt was a lot like him. As a child, Mr. L had always felt like the "dummy" in school and recalled compensating by becoming the class clown. "I always hoped the other kids wouldn't notice that I couldn't do the work if I kept them laughing. It worked pretty good, except that the teachers didn't find me nearly so amusing," he noted ruefully.

Mrs. L was also angry with the school and had been ever since Ned had been barred from the after-school sports program last spring because all of his grades, with the exception of math, were below the necessary "C." She couldn't understand why the school would deprive Ned of the one thing he was good at and why they couldn't do something about the teasing he took at the hands of some of the other boys.

Both parents expressed bewilderment and frustration with Ned's behavior in the family. They desperately wanted to do something that would help Ned be more like his old self but couldn't find a common ground when it came to how to approach the problem. Mr. L worried about how discouraged Ned seemed and felt that Mrs. L tended to be too harsh with him. Mrs. L worried about Ned's unwillingness to work hard in school and felt that her husband babied Ned too much. Both parents worried that between the school problems and the onset of puberty, Ned would become increasingly disobedient and would one day get into some serious trouble.

The psychologist, though, had a suspicion as to why Ned was not progressing. She spent several hours giving Ned a battery of educational and psychological tests. Her findings were conclusive: Ned was clearly dyslexic. He had trouble discriminating between different language sounds, like "ba" and "pa," and he found it almost impossible to do language tasks such as "say 'please' without the 'l'." It seemed that Ned had learned to read by sheer memorization, but this strategy had worked only for a year or two before the task became overwhelming. Ned was able to read lists of words at almost a second-grade level, but when he was asked to decode a list of nonsense words, it was clear he had really weak phonics ("sounding out") skills. He made lots of mistakes involving vowel sounds and had to work really hard to figure out each word.

For a while Ned had been able to hide his reading difficulties by paying good attention in class, but by fourth grade, as the demand for independent work increased and he had to "read to learn," he simply could cope no longer. What he had always thought was "his secret" became apparent to classmates as well. The social fallout from this, with a few hecklers always at his elbow and adults who seemed to think he just wasn't trying, finally overwhelmed him. The psychologist felt that Ned was, indeed, depressed, but that the depression, as well as his acting out, was secondary to the learning disability.

Luckily for Ned, his problems were recognized before they threw his life severely off track. He began to receive special education services in school, in addition to private tutoring at home, to help him succeed despite his dyslexia. Many of his tests were read to him and he was allowed to give the answers orally. On written tests, he was allowed extra time. In social studies, he was given videos and had extra discussions with his teacher to augment the written material and class discussions. His competence at math was highlighted by assigning him to tutor a younger child in basic arithmetic, for which he received a good citizenship award during the spring awards banquet. He was reinstated in the sports program.

Ned and his parents continued to work with the child psychologist, who helped all of them understand Ned's frustration and helped Ned to see his dyslexia within the context of his many strengths. By the end of fifth grade, his behavioral problems were much improved, and he seemed well on his way to becoming the pleasant, cooperative person he had always been.

Thinking about the Case

Dyslexia (known in the *DSM*-IV as reading disorder) is one of several specific developmental disorders (also known as learning disorders) that can be the focus of psychological intervention. The others include difficulties with mathematics or writing or with communicating or motor skills. Specific developmental disabilities are not the same as mental retardation. In fact, learning disabilities such as dyslexia and specific language impairment are generally only diagnosed when the child has roughly normal intelligence. Even intellectually gifted children (like Albert Einstein, for example) can have severe learning disabilities.

It used to be thought that dyslexia occurs much more commonly in boys than in girls. However, more recent research has demonstrated that girls are as likely to have reading problems as boys but that boys are much more likely to be identified as reading disabled because their acting-out behavior makes them the focus of teacher and/or parent attention. Prevalence estimates vary from 1 percent to 10 percent of the population. Since literacy is so important in modern society, dyslexia can constitute a severe occupational, social, and even emotional handicap.

It is generally agreed that dyslexia is primarily a phonological disorder. Dyslexics have trouble discriminating, manipulating, and remembering sounds. Therefore, they have a hard time learning how sounds in the language are represented by letters and how the sounds indicated by the letters in a word should be combined to produce a spoken word. Sometimes dyslexics who have a hard time sounding out written words can learn to recognize them visually. Thus, like Ned, they may be able to memorize several hundred words, but they will be stumped every time they reach an unfamiliar word.

It seems to be the case that dyslexia runs in families. Children whose parents had developmental language disorders or reading problems are at significant risk for dyslexia. Further, individuals who have acquired dyslexia as adults show specific lesions in the posterior part of the left temporal lobe, and a subset of dyslexic children show evidence of abnormal neuronal development in the same area of the brain. However, most do not. Therefore, while it is clear that dyslexia has strong neurological roots, the exact locus or loci of the problem, as well as its causes, are still uncertain.

Like Ned, most learning-disabled children experience at least some accompanying psychological and social problems. Depression and oppositional problems are common. Early diagnosis and intensive intervention are key to preventing these sequelae. While individualized education for disabled students is mandated by law, the quality and availability of special education services vary widely. School psychologists, often overwhelmed by demands for mandated evaluations, may have little time left over for counseling duties. Special education teachers may be asked to teach more students than optimal, due to restricted space or time, and may not have had specific education in the treatment of dyslexia. Parents often find that they must become vocal advocates for their educationally disabled offspring. This can be particularly challenging for parents like Ned's who also may have had problematic educational experiences as youngsters.

The Developmental Perspective

Learning disabilities are probably present from birth but are often not diagnosed until the school years when deficits in specific skills become more apparent. Recent research has demonstrated that an early risk factor for later reading disability is language delay in the preschool period like Ned exhibited.

Many learning-disabled children are identified in first or second grade, but others, like Ned, manage to slip by unnoticed until fourth or fifth grade, when children are assumed to make the shift from "learning to read" to "reading to learn." Some youngsters, such as those with both reading and attentional problems, may be relatively successful through elementary school but may then start showing their disability in middle school, when their lack of organizational and planning skills gets them into difficulty.

Undiagnosed and untreated, learning disabilities can significantly derail future educational, social, psychological, and occupational functioning. Success in school is crucial to a child's future. Self-esteem is dependent on feedback from others, and during the school years teachers and peers are with children for far more hours a day than are parents and may be equally as influential or more influential in shaping a child's self-concept. Being considered "dumb" is horribly stigmatizing and can lead to social withdrawal, identification with a deviant peer group, and decreased motivation and persistence in academic endeavors, as well as depression and anxiety. Thus, a vicious cycle is created: A learning-disabled youngster gradually gives up on academic pursuits, becomes even more academically dysfunctional, and may end by becoming alienated from the mainstream of society.

The problems associated with learning disability may be exacerbated by the onset of adolescence, when demands for competent independent functioning and sensitivity to peer acceptance or rejection are increased. Academically disabled children are then at increased risk for substance abuse and antisocial behavior as their inability to find a successful niche for themselves widens from the school to the larger community. Thus, it is not surprising that a substantial subset of occupationally and socially dysfunctional adults has a history of (often undiagnosed) learning disability in childhood.

Questions to Consider

1. How could Ned's dyslexia have gone unnoticed by parents and teachers for so long? How would an earlier identification have affected this case?

2. If there were a screening tool for learning disabilities, would you

advocate mandating its use across the country? What factors did you consider in coming to your opinion?

3. Do you think that keeping Ned out of after-school sports was a good tactic? Why or why not?

4. Imagine that you and your best friend each had the same specific learning disability. Would you be likely to respond to it differently? How so? How might those differences affect the course of your future?

4

FETAL ALCOHOL SYNDROME:
THE CASE OF ROBBIE A

ROBBIE WAS A funny-looking kid. He was variously described as resembling a "wizened little old man," a "little pixie," and a "little stick of a boy." At age seven, he was smaller than any of the other children in his second-grade class. He had a small mouth and a small pointy chin. His ears looked like they were placed too low on his head. But it was not his looks that were getting Robbie into trouble. It was his behavior.

Robbie's teacher reported that he was always "at other kids" when her back was turned. On the school bus he kicked the kid sitting next to him and ripped books out of the hands of the girl across the aisle. In the cafeteria he wandered around, taking food from trays and poking and teasing whoever would respond. The minute his teacher turned her back in the classroom, he was up out of his chair, climbing on the shelves to reach something he wasn't supposed to have anyway, and when she caught him and told him to get down, he would throw a fit.

Nor did Robbie's academic skills redeem him. He seemed unable to retain new information, "getting" a concept one day and losing it the next. His speech was difficult to understand, and even when the words were comprehensible the meaning might not be. He seemed to jump from thought to thought. He wasn't learning to read very well, and his mathematical skills were well below average. In referring him for evaluation, his teacher commented, "I can tell you right now—I've seen this kind of child before. He's going to wind up in jail . . . or dead."

The school psychologist called Robbie's home to seek parental permission for testing. The phone rang for a long time and was finally answered by a woman's worn, tired, gravelly voice. Mrs. A seemed worried about Robbie's problems and did not hesitate to allow the evaluation. However, when it came time for a parental conference, Mr. A came alone because his wife was not feeling well. Future daytime telephone calls to Robbie's home went unanswered, and the psychologist learned to communicate with Mr. A in the evenings.

Living at home with Robbie were his parents and a nine-year-old nephew of Robbie's, the child of his oldest brother, who was now serving time in jail for grand larceny. Mr. A seemed a bright and reflective man who had had significant trouble holding jobs. He was currently stacking boxes in a warehouse. He related a history of drug and alcohol abuse, which he had gotten under control some five years previously through a stint in rehab and lots of follow-up AA meetings.

His wife, he related, had had a serious alcohol problem for most of her life and was still drinking regularly. She had continued to drink heavily throughout her pregnancies (three in all), and he thought that the guilt about what this might have done to the children served as yet another reason to drink. He knew from his own treatment that nagging her would be of no help, so he was trying to work on his own recovery and carry out his own responsibilities as best he could. He loved his wife and, anyway, he didn't know how he could work and raise the children without her. So separation was really not a consideration.

Testing revealed that Robbie was functioning at a borderline intellectual level. His tested I.Q. was 70. A multidisciplinary team meeting was held, an individualized educational program (IEP) was drawn up, and Robbie was placed in a self-contained special education classroom for behaviorally disturbed youngsters, rather than in a class for slow learners. The adult-to-student ratio was far greater than in the regular classroom. His teacher was strict and unforgiving and had a highly structured approach to learning. While Robbie complained bitterly about how "mean" his teacher was, his behavior improved in this setting, although he continued to have difficulty on the bus and in the cafeteria, where supervision was less available.

Because Mr. A was not always available and his wife was frequently "sick," Robbie had had virtually no supervision with homework. At the school's suggestion, Mr. A arranged for a high school girl who was a neighbor to come in each day to sit with Robbie for one hour each afternoon while he did his homework. She kept him on task (by giving regular reports to his father) and helped him when he got stuck.

While Robbie did better with the additional structure that was being provided for him at home and at school, everyone agreed that his prognosis was guarded. Impulsivity, inadequate self-management skills, and deficits in problem-solving ability were expected to interfere with Robbie's social and academic skill development more or less permanently. The only question was—how much?

Thinking about the Case

Alcohol abuse in women is the third leading cause of birth defects. While fetal alcohol syndrome (FAS) is more often associated with heavy alcohol use during pregnancy, no safe amount of use has been identified. Therefore, the American Medical Association recommends that pregnant women abstain completely from alcohol.

Fetal alcohol syndrome is marked by both physical and behavioral abnormalities. Such infants are usually lighter and smaller than average and may show a range of facial and limb irregularities. Robbie's small, slight build and facial abnormalities are typical of youngsters with FAS. Intelligence is often but not always impaired, as are the capacity for self-control, tolerance for frustration, and sustained attention. Robbie is not unusual, either, in the range of behavioral problems he displays. Youngsters with FAS typically have an extremely difficult time with the demands of school and experience social problems with peers as well.

FAS is not always diagnosed easily. Behavioral problems often are mistaken for attention-deficit hyperactivity disorder (with accompanying learning disabilities or impaired intelligence).

The physical effects of FAS are permanent and are not generally improved much with medication. While a structured environment like the kind Robbie was exposed to at school can be helpful, children with FAS often live in family situations that are relatively chaotic, often due to continuing alcohol abuse in one or more family members. Thus, problems are often compounded by residential instability, inconsistent discipline, family violence, financial stress, and other social disruptions. Family and individual therapies have been attempted with youngsters with FAS, but results are not encouraging. The long-range prognosis is generally fairly gloomy when behavioral and intellectual deficits are severe.

A Developmental Perspective

FAS can be diagnosed at birth when physical symptoms are prominent and the mother's drinking history is known. However, it is often not recognized until a youngster encounters the demands imposed by school. Clearly, the disruptions and disabilities of FAS significantly derail a youngster's intellectual and social development. Inability to delay impulses combined with poor social judgment quickly sets FAS children apart from their peers. They tend to be shunned and disliked. This, in turn, provokes frustration and anger, which can lead to escalating hostility and aggression in interpersonal relationships. Over time, the youngster develops a negative self-image, which contributes to self-identification with social outcasts. Unfortunately, pervasive personality disorder, usually with prominent antisocial symptoms, is not an uncommon outcome.

As the youngster with FAS moves through adolescence, inability to successfully meet the increasing demands for functioning in society causes escalating feelings of failure and frustration. In addition, the increasing availability of drugs and alcohol as the youngster ages increases the risk for impulsive or dangerous behaviors. Many of these youngsters drop out of school and live a marginal existence on the fringes of society. Others come into contact with the law at this point and some will spend the bulk of their young adulthood in and out of jail, as Robbie's teacher prophesied. Further, since FAS affects both size and intelligence, individuals with FAS are at risk of being victimized by larger and more intellectually competent antisocial peers. Those whose deficits are less severe and who experience a high level of structure in their childhood environments may be able to hold nondemanding jobs as adults and to maintain some meaningful interpersonal relationships.

Questions to Consider

1. Might some of Robbie's problems be associated with his mother's continued drinking and inadequate parenting? How might you sort out nature and nurture in this case?

2. What do you think Robbie will be like as an adolescent? Describe how you envision him to be functioning at school and in the world. What about as an adult? How might he be functioning at thirty? At fifty?

3. What steps might society take to reduce the incidence or severity of FAS? Consider both approaches that might help to prevent FAS entirely and those that would lessen its impact on individuals, families, and society.

5

TOURETTE'S DISORDER:
THE CASE OF CHARLIE R

CHARLIE'S HUMMING WAS driving his seventh-grade teachers crazy. In fact, he seemed to be trying to do just that. When they would glare at him, he 'd look anxious and puzzled. When, finally, they hissed or yelled "humming!" he'd stop and mumble "sorry." But the minute their backs were turned, he would start up again. Sometimes Charlie banged on the desk for no apparent reason. His math teacher reported these behaviors to the school psychologist to whom she and other teachers had appealed for help in managing Charlie's behavior. His normally good grades were dropping; he couldn't seem to keep his mind on his work; he was always in motion. His English teacher added, "It's like he's always in overdrive." While some of his peers seemed to enjoy Charlie's high jinks, most were beginning to tease or avoid him.

The psychologist observed Charlie in several of his classes and spoke with his mother. The observations confirmed the behaviors that the teachers had described. Charlie was generally in motion. But she felt that his humming and beating on the desk were unconscious, rather than purposefully attention seeking. In fact, Charlie seemed unhappy and anxious.

The psychologist subsequently learned from Mrs. R that Charlie was an only child. Mrs. R was a secretary and her husband stayed at home due to a back injury that had resulted in a permanent disability. Mrs. R agreed that Charlie had seemed subdued and worried for some months and wondered if he had been one of the children who had bought marijuana from a stranger who had been hanging around the playground at the end of the previous school year.

Interviewing and testing Charlie did not reveal much. He seemed mildly depressed and moderately anxious. He denied involvement in the marijuana incident that had worried his mother. His intelligence was above average and he didn't appear to have any learning disabilities. The psychologist doubted that he had attention-deficit hyperactivity disorder since his symptoms were of recent and relatively sudden onset.

Some months went by, and Charlie again came to the attention of the school psychologist. Apparently in a discussion of suicide overheard by the librarian during study period, Charlie had said, "It's not that easy to kill yourself, you know." He then listed several ways he had tried and failed to cause his own death. He described skateboarding into a brick wall, running into oncoming traffic, and trying to drown himself in the bathtub.

When Charlie met with the psychologist this time, he seemed quite upset. Tearfully, he denied feeling suicidal at present and said that those feelings had occurred months ago. He couldn't remember why he'd felt that way, but he was okay now. He didn't want his mom to know what he had said. He figured she'd be mad at him—again.

Throughout the interview, Charlie cleared his throat over and over. Observing this behavior gave the psychologist a new thought about Charlie's problems. She queried his teachers about whether Charlie displayed any vocal or facial tics. Yes, they reported, he did. Often he made barking noises "just like a little dog." They had each assumed this was one more strategy for annoying them. One teacher insisted that it could not be a tic (which is, by definition, not purposive) because Charlie could "control it when he wanted to." In addition, his math teacher had noticed the appearance of a facial tic when he was concentrating on a math test. She described it as "almost a wink, but with his whole cheek moving as well."

By this time, the school psychologist was convinced that Charlie was suffering from Tourette's syndrome. This diagnosis was quickly confirmed by a pediatric neurologist, who recommended both medication to treat the tics directly and supportive psychotherapy to help Charlie cope better with the effects of the tic disorder on his life, which would in turn reduce the depression he was experiencing.

Unfortunately, Mrs. R, while accepting the diagnosis, did not want her son to take medicine. She was concerned about possible side effects and about the possibility that he would become dependent on the medicine. Nor did she feel that he needed psychotherapy, as his mood seemed fine at home. Instead, she wanted the school administration to make sure that Charlie was not penalized for tic behaviors, since they represented a medical condition. A compromise agreement was reached: Mrs. R would consider medication for Charlie if his tics worsened. He would be allowed to see the school psychologist if he felt upset or depressed. His teachers agreed (some more reluctantly than others) to a system of rewards and incentives to help Charlie stay on task and complete assignments and to stay in close touch with his mother about his progress. But before this plan had time to be tested adequately, Charlie's family moved out of the school district and he was lost to follow-up.

Thinking about the Case

In the late 1800s a French neurologist, Georges Gilles de la Tourette, discovered and named for himself a curious disorder he had recently observed in children under his care. Later, this disorder came to be known informally as "the cursing disease" because some of its sufferers would blurt out profane or obscene words without warning and for no reason.

Tourette's disorder begins before age eighteen and is distinguished by multiple motor and one or more vocal tics. A tic is a sudden, brief, repetitive, stereotyped vocalization or movement. Sounds can include humming, barking, throat clearing, or even specific words. Some examples of motor tics are darting movements of the hands or arms, leg kicking, ankle turning, facial grimaces, and winking. While the tics can be suppressed voluntarily for brief periods of time, they reemerge in bursts after a buildup of internally experienced tension.

Tics may be transient, appearing during times of stress and disappearing as mysteriously as they came. Therefore, a tic disorder is not diagnosed unless the symptoms have been present for more than one year.

Tic disorders, of which Tourette's is one example, are now known to be primarily neurological in origin, although they cause a good deal of psychological distress, as is illustrated by Charlie's experience. In situations in which the tics need to be suppressed, as in school, sufferers are often quite tense and preoccupied. Trying to control the tics for long periods of time is an exhausting and generally fruitless prospect. Like Charlie, sufferers may have difficulty attending to tasks at hand. Experiencing uncontrollable behaviors, particularly when these are unexplained, frequently causes a diminution in self-esteem, as well as a sense of shame and self-stigmatization. These effects are, of course, exacerbated by the reactions of others like Charlie's teachers and peers. Not surprisingly, Tourette's can co-occur with depression or anxiety disorders.

In addition, Tourette's co-occurs at a rate greater than chance with obsessive-compulsive disorder (OCD), leading to the hypothesis that the compulsivity of simple behaviors like tics and complex behaviors like thoughts and handwashing may have a single (or related) neurological origin. Bolstering this hypothesis is the fact that Tourette's, OCD, and depression can all be treated with the same class of medications, the selective serotonin reuptake inhibitors (SSRIs).

Optimism about the prognosis for Tourette's has increased in the last decade with the availability of new medications. Previously, psychodynamic psychotherapy was the treatment of choice, but its success rate was abysmal. Now medication, education about the diagnosis and its implications for the individual and family members (as well as teachers and significant others), and supportive psychotherapy designed to reduce the secondary effects of the tic disorder on the person's self-concept and functioning are generally parts of a comprehensive treatment plan. The manifestations of the disorder can be largely controlled. However, the medication suppresses, rather than cures, symptoms. It must be taken continuously, or the patient is likely to relapse.

The Developmental Perspective

Tics can emerge at any time during childhood. The important consideration, from a psychological standpoint, is how quickly the tics are diagnosed and treated. Untreated tic disorder can single a child out for teasing or shunning, as it did with Charlie. Diminution of self-esteem and depression are then likely. Opportunities for social learning and growth are impaired. These effects worsen markedly in adolescence when youngsters more acutely feel the need for acceptance by peers. Clearly, the later the intervention, the worse it is for the child.

Tics can interfere with mastering developmental tasks in the academic arena as well. Since tics are often accompanied by a general increase in the level of tension, and since the attempt to suppress the tics in school increases tension still further, youngsters with these disorders tend to be distractible and irritable. Thus, untreated tic disorder can produce deficits in self-concept, social development, and learning.

Questions to Consider

1. Can Tourette's be a completely neurological phenomenon if one of its symptoms is blurting out forbidden words? Speculate on what might be some possible causes for this interesting symptom.

2. Like Charlie's mother, many parents are wary of medication and/or of allowing their child to have a "private" psychotherapy relationship with another adult. Do you believe there are any circumstances when parents should be compelled to cooperate with medically prescribed treatment? Do you think that Charlie's mother's behavior constituted "medical neglect," which would warrant intervention by the department of social services? Justify your answer.

3. Tourette's is an example of a neurological illness with substantial psychological and social sequelae. Have you or a family member or friend ever had an injury or illness that had psychological or social effects? What were they, and why did they come about? What does this tell you about the applicability of the biopsychosocial model to "physical" illness?

PART TWO

Anxiety and
Somatoform Disorders

———◄O►———

Nine-month-old children are afraid of strangers. Three-year-olds are afraid of the dark or of the monster that lurks in the closet. Five-year-olds get stomachaches before beginning kindergarten. Adolescents worry about their appearance, whether they are in the right crowd, what college they should go to. Fears and anxieties are common among youngsters, as they are among adults. Sometimes these fears and anxieties create havoc in the lives of sufferers, interfering with their ability to carry out their normal daily activities. In these cases an anxiety disorder may be diagnosed. What does anxiety look like in children of different ages? Why do some youngsters master fear while others are consumed by it? How can anxious or fearful children be helped to lead a more normal life?

To explore these questions we have included five cases of anxiety disorder in this section. In the first, a five-year-old youngster suffers from such a wide range of fears that he is virtually incapacitated. In the second, feelings of panic cause a girl to refuse to go to school. The third case illustrates obsessive-compulsive disorder, a disorder in which a person has unpleasant, sometimes bizarre, ideas pop into his mind. In reaction, he often feels compelled to engage in various seemingly nonsensical rituals, sometimes for hours a day. The last two cases examine the lingering effects of trauma in youngsters of two different ages.

While most of the cases in this section illustrate expressed anxiety, we have also included one case to represent the category of somatoform disorders in which anxiety may be inferred rather than expressed. Somatoform disorders include those in which the presence of physical symptoms suggests an underlying medical condition but the medical condition either is not found or does not fully account for the level of functional impairment. These conditions have been inadequately researched in children, so their prevalence and developmental course are still poorly understood. The case included here concerns a preadolescent youngster who has a variety of unexplained physical symptoms in the context of both familial and peer stressors. It poses the interesting question of how it might be that psychological distress sometimes is expressed as physical symptoms.

6

GENERALIZED ANXIETY DISORDER:
THE CASE OF MATTHEW Q

MATTHEW WAS A BRIGHT, engaging five-year-old boy who was virtually incapacitated by fears. His mother brought him to a child psychologist because he had become preoccupied with concerns about death, expressing fears that he or his parents or grandparents would die, asking questions about death, and asking about who in their family had died. Apparently, his anxieties had been triggered by the recent death of his grandparents' dog.

In the first evaluation session, Matthew and his parents reported a variety of fears. For the past several years, Matthew had been afraid to sleep in his own room. Although he would sometimes go to bed in his own bed, he insisted that his mother or father lie down in the bed next to him until he fell asleep. Almost invariably, he woke up at about 2 A.M. and insisted on spending the rest of the night in his parents' bed. Matthew was also frightened by a "poison control" sticker on the kitchen door, a security alarm near his front door, and a crucifix at his grandmother's house.

Matthew was also very afraid of thunderstorms. Whenever it threatened to rain, he would refuse to go outside and he insisted on staying close to his mother or father. Matthew was so focused on his fear of thunderstorms that he routinely turned on the Weather Channel to see if storms were expected in the area.

In addition, Matthew was excessively timid about engaging in physical activities. This interfered significantly with his mastery of age-appropriate skills like going on the slide, seesaw, swing, or jungle gym. As a result he was often teased by other children, who called him "sissy" and "wimp."

Not surprisingly, Matthew also experienced intense separation anxiety. Although he was one of the oldest children in his pre-kindergarten class (his parents had delayed his entry into kindergarten because of concerns about his social maturity), he had developed a severe separation problem in the weeks preceding his entrance into therapy. He insisted that his mother either remain in the classroom or spend the morning in a room down the hall. When his mother tried to leave, Matthew went into a severe panic reaction and cried uncontrollably.

The psychologist hypothesized that Matthew's extensive array of fears was shaped by both constitutional and experiential factors, involving a complex and dynamic interplay of biological predispositions, parental modeling, and child-rearing experiences. On the constitutional side, in addition to being acutely perceptive, imaginative, and verbal, Matthew was extremely anxious by temperament. He was physically timid, hesitant to try new activities, and slow to develop confidence in physical or social skills. Perhaps in reaction to how stressful he found his world, he was prone to a variety of physical ailments, such as colds, allergies, diarrhea, and vomiting.

Interestingly, Matthew's mother had suffered from a severe school phobia as a teenager but she had recovered fully after a short course of therapy. She reported being very close to her parents, who lived a few blocks away. She spoke to them at least daily and they visited together at least once each weekend, generally after they had all gone to Mass on Saturday evening. Although Matthew's father had no history of anxiety problems, his wife joked about how he was always following her around in the kitchen and cleaning things off.

As the beloved only child of devoted parents, it was natural that Matthew was the center of attention most of the time. His parents were extremely sensitive to his moods, solicitous of his feelings, attentive to his conversation, and indulgent with his whims and demands. However, Matthew's parents were even more concerned about his health than most loving parents. They worried whenever he became even slightly ill, keeping him home from school when he seemed "under the weather."

Inadvertently, Matthew's parents may have contributed to his fears of physical activity. It emerged later that Matthew had fallen off his changing table when he was about nine months old. His parents had taken him to the emergency room, where they learned that no significant injury had occurred. However, ever since, they had worried that Matthew would fall and hurt himself and so had been cautious about letting him explore playground equipment.

As therapy unfolded, it became clear that Matthew's parents had instinctively and systematically shielded him from anything unpleasant or scary. For instance, they had never talked to him about his maternal great-grandfather's death a few years after his birth. When the therapist asked whether or not Matthew had learned about death from children's books such as *Babar,* his parents explained that they had always expurgated such content when reading stories to him. In a well-intentioned but perhaps misguided attempt to protect him from potentially upsetting material they had prevented Matthew from learning about and developing strategies for coping with life's painful realities.

Therapy unfolded on a number of fronts, each of which involved the parents as active collaborators in all interventions. Children's books were used to help Matthew learn about and face issues related to illness and death. The therapist read with Matthew a collection of books about illness, the human body, death of pets and loved ones, and disputes over postdeath outcome. Matthew reacted with great interest and would often come into therapy and ask the therapist to read one of his favorite parts, such as when Babar has a nightmare on the day the old lady is bitten by a snake and old Cornelius is injured in a house fire.

Meanwhile, Matthew's parents were gradually exposing him to feared situations in the outside world. Repeated exposure to fear-evoking stimuli was reinforced by dinosaur stickers and by enthusiastic praise from his parents and therapist for his increasing mastery of fear. Gradually, the stickers were phased out as Matthew began to take pride in his growing ability to cope with anxiety. About six months into treatment, Matthew's therapist gave him a small photo album with snapshots of about twenty situations he had once feared and had now mastered.

Matthew's parents were counseled to allow Matthew to watch the Weather Channel for only ten minutes a day. At the same time, they helped him to learn more about thunderstorms, thereby channeling some of his anxiety into the intellectual activity of learning about thunder and lightning and developing a more realistic appraisal of the dangers associated with storms. To his parents' great surprise, Matthew's sleep problems resolved very quickly when they initiated a positive reinforcement system whereby he could earn a small toy soldier every night he slept in his own bed until 7 A.M.

Since Matthew's anxiety about separating from his mother was directly related to his insecurity about acceptance by his peers, social skills training also played a role in treatment. Modeling, encouragement, and reinforcement were used in the classroom by his teacher to help Matthew develop more appropriate interactive behaviors. Here again he was encouraged to confront and master his fears, rather than retreat and be overwhelmed by them.

By the end of treatment, which lasted about nine months, Matthew was sleeping in his own bed, attending school without difficulty, getting together for "play dates," and riding a two-wheeler. He was very proud of how well he had done on his "job" of overcoming his fears. Although Matthew remained a child more timid than bold, more tense than relaxed, he had learned to deal with realities like death, thunderstorms, and separation from his parents, and he was excited about the prospect of starting kindergarten at the "big school" shortly after his sixth birthday.

Thinking about the Case

Generalized anxiety disorder, which is marked by chronically excessive anxiety and worry, is found in people of all ages, although it is more commonly diagnosed in adolescents than in younger children. While its prevalence in the population is between 2 percent and 3 percent, it accounts for over 20 percent of the problems for which parents seek clinical treatment for their children. It is diagnosed more frequently in females than males across a variety of cultures.

Matthew has symptoms illustrating each of the four elements of anxiety. He has cognitive components; for example, he evaluates thunderstorms and playing on the playground as more dangerous than they actually are. He voices a number of somatic complaints, chiefly digestive problems of various sorts. He suffers from classic emotional symptoms of dread, tension, and worry; he is hypervigilant about danger. Finally, he shows the behavioral components of escape and avoidance.

As it does in the other anxiety disorders, heritability plays a role in the genesis of general anxiety disorder. Note that Matthew's mother suffered from a school phobia as a youngster. Her intense attachment to her mother may be symptomatic of separation problems as well. His father appears to have a mildly phobic response to disorder, although nothing that any of us would consider "clinically abnormal." When an anxious temperament is combined with conditioning of anxiety (for example, being teased by other children), parental modeling of anxious responses, or reinforcement of avoidant or anxious behavior, the groundwork is laid for the development of a more persistent anxiety disorder.

Treatment for generalized anxiety disorder includes medication and cognitive-behavioral therapy. Antianxiety medications have been shown to clearly reduce anxiety during the time that the medication is taken. However, the risk of relapse is high once the medication is withdrawn, and antianxiety medications all have a high potential for abuse and addiction. Cognitive-behavioral therapy has also been shown to be effective, with more lasting gains than medication. Matthew's treatment was essentially cognitive-behavioral in orientation, focusing on his beliefs and thoughts and emphasizing behavioral assignments and goals.

The prognosis for generalized anxiety disorder is generally considered guarded. While the subclinical, normal fears of childhood disappear over time, generalized anxiety tends to be more chronic, particularly if it is part of a family pattern of anxiety disorders. Most patients improve to some extent with treatment, but few are "cured." The majority experience weeks or months at a time when the symptoms are better and other periods when they are worse. Of course, external stress will exacerbate the condition.

The Developmental Perspective

All children have fears. Between the ages of birth and about two, fears of noises, strange persons, and objects tend to predominate. By four, most of these have dissipated, to be replaced by fears of imaginary creatures, robbers, and the dark. As children age, they develop the capacity to conceptualize the future and thus have more future-oriented worries—for example, that their parents will get hurt or divorced, or that they will fail at some goal. Not surprisingly, adolescents tend to worry about whether they are smart enough, funny enough, thin enough, or cool enough. Performance and acceptance are the areas on which their anxieties come to rest.

Generalized anxiety disorder is more common in adolescents than in younger children. In addition, older youngsters with this disorder tend to have a greater number of symptoms and more co-morbidity. That is, they are more likely to suffer from depression or behavioral problems associated with their anxiety. While younger children have to deal only with the anxiety itself, adolescents have to deal with the anxiety and also with the self-image deficits produced by the anxiety. It is one thing to have some fears; it is quite another to think of oneself as a fearful person, particularly in adolescence when fearlessness is valued more highly than at any other developmental stage.

Not surprisingly, generalized anxiety disorder interferes with mastering a host of important skills. Motor behaviors may lag if youngsters, like Matthew, are afraid of learning new skills such as riding a bike or swimming. Further, when anxiety disorder begins in earlier childhood, youngsters tend to have more social impairment than when they have gone through their preadolescent years without clinically significant anxiety.

Questions to Consider

1. Can you identify the processes of classical and instrumental conditioning in the development of any of Matthew's fears?
2. If you were the parent of a timid child like Matthew what steps might you take to inoculate him against the development of an anxiety disorder? How confident are you that your strategies would be successful? Why?
3. What are some reasons that generalized anxiety disorder might be diagnosed less frequently in males than in females?

7

SCHOOL REFUSAL:
THE CASE OF ROSEANNE A

ROSEANNE WAS AN ATTRACTIVE ten-year-old girl, the middle of three children born to Mr. A, a psychiatrically disabled Vietnam veteran, and Mrs. A, a nursing home administrator. The family lived on a fifty-acre farm that had been in Mrs. A's family for generations. While Mrs. A worked, Mr. A stayed home and tended to the house and large garden. He suffered from anxiety, depression, and difficulty controlling his temper, as well as a deep distrust of authority of all kinds. For this reason, he had difficulty interacting with people and left home only when he had to and only for brief periods of time. As long as he was given lots of space and avoided stressful situations, he did fairly well. His family seemed to accept his limitations with good grace, and he, in turn, was as loving a father as he was able to be. All three children were excellent students and were well liked by their peers. Roseanne was active in school activities and particularly loved the pre-cheerleader program that she hoped would lead to the real thing when she got to junior high school.

Shortly after fourth grade began, Roseanne began missing a lot of school. She complained of stomachaches, headaches, and fatigue. By mid-October, she had already missed ten days, and the teacher suggested that the family seek a medical opinion. Despite blood tests and a thorough exam, no definitive diagnosis could be rendered. The physician wondered whether Roseanne might be suffering from chronic fatigue syndrome. In the meantime, the symptoms seemed to be worsening, and by December, Roseanne was complaining that she was being hassled by teachers and friends about her absences.

Mr. A, who was beginning to be exasperated by the school's continued insistence that the parents do something about Roseanne's attendance problem, suggested that since he was home anyway, he would home-school Roseanne for the rest of the school year with the view toward having her return to school in September.

Things seemed to go well as long as Roseanne was home-schooled. She continued to be active in after-school activities and to be busy with her friends on weekends. However, her return to school in September went poorly, and again her parents took her out and resumed home schooling. This time, though, Roseanne began to have difficulty going to her outside activities. She complained that her friends were making fun of her and she began to avoid them. At home, where she spent more and more time, she seemed moody and blue.

At this point, worried about Roseanne's generalized withdrawal and apparent unhappiness, her parents sought a second medical opinion about the diagnosis of chronic fatigue syndrome. The second pediatrician suggested that Roseanne's behavior was suggestive of school phobia, particularly in the absence of any medical evidence of organic problems. She referred the family to a psychologist, who, in concert with the parents and school psychologist, developed a plan to gradually reintroduce Roseanne to school.

Over the summer, Mr. and Mrs. A took Roseanne to school several times a week, walking the halls with her, having her show them the cafeteria, the gym, and the library, and helping her find her sixth-grade classroom. It was agreed that her sixth-grade teacher would pick her up each day and personally take her to school. Her parents agreed to the criteria for staying home: a fever of 100.5°F, or vomiting with accompanying signs of illness.

For the first three weeks of school, everything went fine. Then the excuses started: The teachers were talking about her behind her back; her friends were teasing her; her stomachaches had returned. One day toward the end of September, as Mr. A was trying to get her into the car to go to school, Roseanne had what her father described as a "hissy fit." She hung on to the car doors, braced her legs, cried, and pleaded with her father not to make her go. Mr. A reported that Roseanne had seemed completely panicked and out of control, and he could not bring himself to force her when she seemed so genuinely frightened.

While Roseanne was still not verbalizing any symptoms of panic, only that she "hated school," the treatment team suspected that she might have an underlying panic disorder and approached this disorder in three ways: First, her pediatrician prescribed a trial of an antidepressant that is also used to treat panic disorder; second, the psychologist began to educate the family about panic disorder; and third, the psychologist taught Roseanne controlled breathing, relaxation strategies, and cognitive techniques for reducing anxiety.

Interestingly, Mr. A, upon hearing about the symptoms of panic disorder, admitted that he had experienced these ever since his Vietnam experience, and in fact, they were implicated in his inability to work. He was unable to drive more than thirty miles from home and avoided crowded restaurants, movie theaters, the mall, and church. He only really felt safe at home and had to "recuperate" there when he'd been out ferrying the children around or making a quick trip to the grocery store.

Roseanne managed to make it through the end of the school year with a greater than average but acceptable number of absences. She resumed her cheerleading and social activities, and her mood seemed improved, although she was not quite back to her old self. Her parents, who did not want her to be on medication any longer than necessary, took her off the antidepressant in June and the summer went by uneventfully. But by October of the next school year, she began again to deteriorate. This time, Roseanne was able to verbalize what she was feeling. She reported feeling sweaty and hot, with a beating heart and difficulty breathing. She said that she felt like she was going to die. These symptoms occurred in anticipation of going to school and several times during the course of a school day. These are some of the classic symptoms of panic attack.

Medication was quickly resumed and a plan was developed to again gradually increase Roseanne's class time. At first, she had unlimited access to the nurse's office when she felt anxious. This was gradually reduced over a period of weeks as the medication took hold and as she worked to manage the anxiety she did experience.

Roseanne did reasonably well over the next several years with the help of medication and with the use of the skills she had been taught by her psychologist. She still missed more school days than most kids, but she kept up academically, her mood was fairly stable, and her social relationships improved. In ninth grade, she elected to again try school without medicine and she did well for about a year. When she experienced occasional attacks of anxiety she would use her coping techniques to manage them successfully. In tenth grade, she restarted medication on her own when the attacks worsened and caused her to miss school. By now, she had gotten pretty savvy about the disorder and knew to intervene early before her avoidance behavior became strongly entrenched.

Interestingly, Roseanne's younger sister began to have similar symptoms when she reached the same age as Roseanne had been when her problems started. Her parents wondered whether Cindy might have modeled or imitated her sister's problems, but she, too, was started on medication and rapidly became symptom-free. She had no further difficulty with school attendance at all.

Thinking about the Case

About 1 percent of youngsters have serious difficulty attending school at some point. Often the problem begins after the child has been out of school for a while due to vacation or illness. School phobia is distinguishable from truancy in that the truant child reports disliking school, has low achievement, often engages in other antisocial behaviors, and skips school without parents' knowledge. The phobic child, on the other hand, usually does well academically, expresses a great deal of anxiety about attendance, and stays home with the knowledge and consent of parents. School refusal of any kind often leads to serious academic and social difficulties in childhood and is associated with increased risk for anxiety disorders, job difficulties, and personality disorder in adulthood, so prompt and effective treatment is imperative.

School phobia is generally a multidimensional phenomenon. Predisposition to panic attacks can be inherited. Mr. A suffered from agoraphobia, a disorder marked by avoidance of situations in which escape might be difficult or help unavailable in the event of symptoms of panic. His agoraphobia had developed gradually in response to panic attacks he had suffered upon returning from Vietnam. Roseanne's sister also had them but was treated quickly and thus did not develop significant avoidance behavior. This family's story is instructive in illustrating the differences in outcome when panic disorder is treated quickly and decisively (as it was in Cindy's case), after some diagnostic confusion (as it was with Roseanne), or not at all (as was the case, sadly, with Mr. A).

Temperamental traits such as timidity or shyness, exacerbated by delayed maturation, often lay a physiological groundwork for school phobia. Psychological factors can include an unusually high level of aspiration accompanied by fear of failure or fears about social rejection or even physical attack. A child may experience concerns about parental fighting or illness, leading to separation anxiety when the child must be away from parents.

Environmental influences are also common. Sometimes, a parent has a high level of anxiety. His fears about the child's safety and well-being when away from him (or his fears about his own ability to be away from his child) can get communicated to the youngster. It is possible that this modeling effect played some role in the development of Roseanne's avoidance behaviors. Also, parents may inadvertently reinforce school avoidant behaviors by allowing the child to watch television or play video games or by being attentive and solicitous to the child who is home from school. After all, it is quite natural to comfort a child who appears ill or frightened.

In any case, multimodal treatment works best, and this approach involves close cooperation between physician, psychologist, parents, and school personnel, as illustrated in this case. First, parents are encouraged to apply pressure on the child to return to school, to set clear guidelines about when he or she may stay home, and to refrain from rewarding school-refusing behavior. Children are taught strategies for relaxing and mastering anxiety and are encouraged to practice these in the school setting. This is essentially the same behavioral treatment applied to any phobia: Exposure to the feared situation is paired with anxiety-reducing techniques. If the child or parent has unrealistic aspirations or fears, cognitive therapy can be helpful in reducing cognitive distortions that maintain anxiety and in "reframing" situations so that they produce less discomfort. A child can learn, for example, that no catastrophe accompanies getting less than straight A's or playing a trumpet solo less well than hoped for. A youngster who is subject to teasing can develop more assertive responses that give the child some sense of control and can use humor to counteract a sense of shame. Sometimes, antidepressants or antianxiety medications are prescribed to reduce physiological symptoms of panic, so that the child's mastery strategies are more likely to be effective. In general, the more immediate the intervention, and the greater the cooperation between therapist, parents, and school, the better the prognosis.

The Developmental Perspective

We have already mentioned that delayed social maturation might be implicated in the onset of school phobia in young children. Rather than pushing a young child into school, therapists will advise parents to wait a year to enroll an unduly shy or fearful child. Likewise, the anxious parent can usually be supported through the child's entrance into school. In any case, her cooperation is easily enlisted as she knows she must get her child into school; failure to do so reflects on her competence as a parent.

As children age, more and more factors can come into play, complicating the picture. Social ridicule, fear of failure, or the development of panic symptoms may accumulate over time. Adolescents with school avoidance are generally less responsive to treatment than are younger children. Perhaps this is partially because parents can exert less actual control over the youngster's behavior as he or she ages. It is virtually impossible to physically compel an adolescent to attend school without drawing the attention of local child protective authorities. Parents often express frustration accompanied by a strong sense of helplessness in relating to their adolescent school refuser, whereas parents of younger children are more able to adopt a posture of firm support.

In addition, unconscious, psychological defense mechanisms designed to protect the individual from anxiety develop gradually throughout childhood. To whatever extent resistance to adult authority, striving toward autonomy, and difficulty expressing weakness or fear are part of normal development, adolescents would have greater ability to rationalize or redefine the school phobia as an expression of individual choice than would younger children. To be afraid of school is to leave oneself open for ridicule and contempt, whereas to refuse to go to school is to assert one's courage and individuality. For example, small children who are being tormented by a bully will fairly readily tell their parents, who can then intervene to help them, whereas older youngsters will try to handle the situation themselves—with school phobia as one possible outcome. For adolescents to be treated successfully, internal motivation to participate actively in treatment and return to school is critical, whereas parental motivation and competence are generally enough to resolve the problem in younger children.

Questions to Consider

1. Would you consider Roseanne's treatment a success? Why or why not? Are there any elements of treatment you would have added to try to improve the outcome?

2. Offer a behavioral explanation for why school phobia often initially appears after an absence from school. Can you counter this with a psychodynamic or family systems explanation? Which do you find most compelling? Why?

3. Consider the possibility of designing a demonstration project to protect at-risk youngsters from developing school refusal. What criteria might you use to choose the children for the project? What interventions would you incorporate? Why?

8

OBSESSIVE-COMPULSIVE DISORDER:
THE CASE OF BEN B

BEN WAS ALMOST twelve years old, but he looked like he was nine. A small, redheaded youngster with furrowed brow, he scanned my office with anxious eyes. At his request, his mother had accompanied him to the interview, and at her urging he told me his problem.

"I have to touch corners," he said. "Like when I come into a room, I have to touch where the door meets the wall. And when I walk by a desk at school, I have to touch the corner of the desk. If I get called up to the front of the class, I have to touch each desk going up and each desk coming back. It's making me crazy. I can't stand it!"

"He started this about four months ago," his mother added. "I've suggested he just try to stop, but he gets almost hysterical and says he just can't. I've tried to reward him when he goes through a door without touching it, and I've tried punishing him when he does. Nothing seems to help. Lately he's doing it all the time, sometimes going back to touch the same place again and again. I'm at my wits' end!"

"Don't you think I'd stop it if I could?" Ben was crying now. "I have to do it or something really bad will happen. Somebody will get hurt really bad."

"Who might get hurt, Ben?" I asked.

"I don't know. Mom or Dad, or maybe my sister or my teacher. Somebody I know."

"Tell the doctor about the other part, Ben," urged Mrs. B.

"I have to hold my breath if I see anything bad," he whispered, head in his hands.

"Can you tell me more about that?"

"Well, it's like if I'm watching a movie and I see the bad guy, then I have to hold my breath until I see something good. If somebody says a bad word at school I have to hold my breath until I hear something good."

"What happens if you start to run out of breath before someone says something good?" I asked.

"I can say something good in my head and it counts. I say a prayer usually or I think something nice about somebody," he answered.

By this time, within the first ten minutes of the interview, the diagnosis was clear: Ben had obsessive-compulsive disorder (OCD).

Ben was the younger of two children in a middle-class family. His father was a guard at the local prison. Mrs. B described her husband as a good man whose stutter had made him somewhat shy and wary of social situations. He'd spent a lot of time with Ben, though, fishing and hunting. Mrs. B was a dental hygienist at a local office. She worked part time so that one parent could always be home with Ben and his older sister, Karen.

Mrs. B added that Karen had had some learning difficulties and was getting extra help with reading and math. She had been diagnosed at one time with attention-deficit hyperactivity disorder, but the medication that had been prescribed did not agree with her and had been discontinued.

Apparently, Ben's symptoms had developed gradually over several months. Mrs. B felt that the death of her father almost eight months before might have been a precipitating stressor. She and her husband had been particularly close to her dad since Mr. B's father had died when he was a youngster. Mr. B had been sort of "adopted" by her dad and so she and her husband and the children had each felt the loss keenly. She didn't think that she was entirely over it and wondered if her sadness and diminished interest in her usual activities had affected Ben adversely.

As a little guy, Ben had been subjected to his share of teasing. He described not having very many friends, and those he did have were a year or two younger than he was. He still liked comics and superheroes, while many of his age mates were into school sports and girls. He enjoyed his time with his father and, indeed, missed his grandfather very much. He voiced a good bit of anxiety about what happened to people when they died, and apparently his parents' explanations about heaven and hell hadn't reassured him.

In general, Ben appeared to be a somewhat anxious youngster of above-average intelligence with a wide, although somewhat developmentally delayed, range of interests. He was eating and sleeping normally, could laugh at a joke, and was warmly attached to his loved ones.

Once the diagnosis of obsessive-compulsive disorder had been made, Ben was referred to his pediatrician for treatment with clomipramine, a medication that has been shown to decrease the symptoms of this disorder. Psychotherapy focused at first on helping Ben articulate and master some of his anxieties. He learned how to be more assertive with peers who teased him and how to relax his muscles if he became anxious. He talked a lot about what happened after death and about how fearful hell seemed to him to be. With his parents' help he decided that hell was reserved for a few really bad people and that people who made normal mistakes and tried to do better would go to heaven. He seemed particularly comforted by the idea that people who went to heaven would be reunited with their loved ones who had also died.

After a few weeks on medicine, the compulsions to touch corners and hold his breath had diminished but not disappeared. At this point, Ben agreed to work with his therapist on reducing these behaviors. For most of each therapy hour, they walked in and out of the office over and over while Ben kept his hands in his pockets to keep from touching all the corners. Ben dealt with his anxiety by talking about it as he experienced it and by using the relaxation techniques that his therapist had taught him. He also practiced reminding himself that nothing terrible would happen if he inhibited the compulsions, that the urge to do them was a "false alarm" that his brain was sending and not really a signal of danger.

Ben's father was enlisted as the therapist's proxy for home practice sessions, and this provoked an interesting insight that Mr. B shared with me after the first week of practice. He reported remembering that he, too, had had some irrational compulsions off and on throughout his life. For example, he had had to adjust the shower temperature three times before getting in and he had had to pat the dog in multiples of three as well. These compulsions had come and gone throughout his life, and he had never paid them very much attention before. They had seemed like silly, minor quirks that he could stop if he'd wanted to, but they'd given him some kind of comfort at the time, so he just did them until they faded away on their own.

The combination of medication and practice sessions had the desired effect over the next three months of treatment. By this time, Ben had stopped touching and holding his breath, although he could detect, from time to time, that the urge was still there. At those times, he would pay attention to inhibiting the behaviors and remind himself of the "false alarm." Mr. and Mrs. B elected to continue Ben in treatment with a new goal of helping him with his social anxiety and immaturity. Ben's OCD symptoms remained under good control despite a gradual tapering and discontinuation of medication over the five years in which I remained in contact with his family.

Thinking about the Case

Obsessive-compulsive disorder has two parts: (1) obsessions, which are involuntary, recurrent, intrusive thoughts, impulses, or images that cause the individual significant distress, and (2) compulsions, which are illogical or excessive repetitive physical or mental acts that the person feels compelled to perform in order to ward off some dreaded event. The individual usually has both, although only one of the two is necessary for a diagnosis to be made. OCD is distinguished from obsessive-compulsive personality disorder, which describes an individual who is excessively perfectionistic, rigid, and stubborn. In OCD, the symptoms are experienced as unwanted and alien, whereas in obsessive-compulsive personality disorder, the symptoms are experienced by the person as a normal, and in fact laudable, aspect of his or her personality. It used to be thought that this personality disorder was a risk factor or marker for OCD, but the two disorders seem to occur independently and co-occur only occasionally.

OCD seems to be an exaggeration of an everyday phenomenon. Each of us can remember situations where we couldn't get a thought out of our minds: Maybe I didn't turn the stove off; maybe I will fail this test; maybe my mother will have a heart attack. We experience a mild emergency reaction, a sense of foreboding and dread. Most of us are able to distract or calm ourselves and the thought passes. Rituals that ward off anxiety are also common in everyday life: Don't walk under a ladder, "step on a crack and break your mother's back," check the doors and windows before you go to bed, wear your lucky socks to football games, and on and on. Again, most of us recover quickly from the generally mild anxiety that occurs if we are prevented from performing our rituals.

Individuals with OCD experience the obsessions and compulsions as out of control and overpoweringly strong. They are unable to distract themselves from the thoughts or tolerate the anxiety associated with inhibiting the behaviors. Often as the disorder progresses the compulsive rituals take up more and more time, sometimes occupying the sufferer for several hours a day and interfering with normal activities like working and socializing. Typically, the individual experiences the symptoms as shameful and tries to hide them. Many are so successful that OCD may not be diagnosed for years after symptoms first emerge.

OCD occurs in about 2 percent to 3 percent of the population, attacking men and women about equally. The onset is usually gradual, as it was with Ben, and can occur in youngsters as young as three or four or as late as mid-adulthood. Once it occurs, OCD tends to wax and wane, with weeks or months or even years of increased obsessions and rituals interspersed with periods of relative calm.

Obsessive-compulsive disorder frequently co-occurs with other anxiety disorders and with depression. Whether the OCD symptoms cause the sufferer to become depressed or there is a common biological pathway is uncertain, although, interestingly, the medications that are used to control OCD symptoms also are highly effective antidepressants.

Research has indicated that OCD is associated with changes in the functioning of certain areas of the brain, the "cortical-striatal-thalamic" circuit, composed of the caudate nucleus, the orbito-frontal cortex, and the cingulate cortex. These areas appear to be implicated in filtering out irrelevant information and in perseveration of behavior. When patients with OCD are treated successfully with medication, activity in these areas of the brain decreases. Other evidence for the biochemical basis of OCD can be found in its heritability (it tends to run in families) and in its co-morbidity with neurological disorders such as epilepsy and Tourette's syndrome and with brain trauma.

Obsessive-compulsive disorder can be successfully treated in one of two ways. The first is medication. Over half the patients treated with clomipramine, one of the selective serotonin reuptake inhibitors (SSRIs) that are used to treat depression, improve over a period of four to eight weeks. However, medication controls symptoms; it does not cure the disorder. When the medication is withdrawn, symptoms often recur.

The second mode of treatment is behavioral. Compulsive responses are extinguished by a combination of modeling, flooding, and response prevention. If the person can remain in the anxiety-producing situation over an extended period of time without engaging in the compulsive behaviors, the anxiety will gradually extinguish. Interestingly, research indicates that both medication and cognitive-behavioral psychotherapy result in reduced activity in the caudate nucleus of the brain as shown on positron emission tomography (PET) scans.

The treatment of Ben's need to touch corners included these techniques as he and the therapist walked in and out of doorways with

Ben keeping his hands in his pockets. Note that in Ben's case, the therapist added simultaneous relaxation training so that the anxiety response would be more quickly extinguished and so that Ben would feel some sense of control over his reactions. She also included cognitive reframing techniques in which Ben learned to think of his anxiety and need to touch corners as a "false alarm" from his brain.

Behavioral and cognitive-behavioral techniques have been shown to be highly effective in the treatment of compulsions. Approximately two-thirds of patients treated with them improve, and only 10 percent relapse after treatment. However, behavioral techniques are less effective in treating obsessions, since there is no voluntary response to inhibit. "Thought stopping," in which the person shouts "stop!" in his head and then replaces the obsessive thought with a relaxing thought, is mildly helpful for some patients. Interestingly, though, obsessions tend to decrease on their own when compulsions are decreased. In general, behavioral therapy should always be a part of treatment when compulsions are present. When only obsessions are present, medication, along with education about the disorder, may be the treatment of choice.

The Developmental Perspective

Children are naturally superstitious, and warding-off rituals are a natural part of childhood. Some children check under the bed for monsters before they go to sleep; others avoid stepping on cracks in the sidewalk. Primitive people are also superstitious, engaging in numerous rituals designed to provide a sense of control over their enigmatic environment. As adulthood (and science) provides a greater sense of understanding and control over events, superstitious rituals tend to decrease. Therefore, OCD may be somewhat more difficult to diagnose in children.

The content of obsessions tends to widen somewhat over the life span. For example, religious or sexual obsessions are common in adults but rare in children, whereas obsessions about dirt and contamination and counting/checking compulsions are equally common across age groups.

Otherwise, OCD is remarkably similar in symptoms, treatment, and course, regardless of the age of onset. There are no data to suggest that earlier age of onset leads to worse prognosis as it does with many other disorders, although co-morbid neurological conditions like learning difficulties or Tourette's disorder can complicate the youngster's adjustment to school.

Questions to Consider

1. It has been suggested that control (or lack thereof) of life events might be relevant to the timing of onset and exacerbations of OCD. Do you see evidence for this hypothesis in Ben's case?

2. What would you consider Ben's risk factors for the development of OCD? Look at your list. Do the factors you have identified support a "nature" or a "nurture" model of the disorder?

3. It has been pointed out that the specific content of OCD is not arbitrary. Obsessions center around contamination, violence, and vulnerability, whereas compulsive behaviors involve checking and preventive rituals. What are some reasons why this might be so? Do your hypotheses support a biomedical or a psychosocial model for the disorder?

4. Most people retain some superstitious thinking and behavior into adulthood. Observe and inquire of yourself and your friends in this regard. What did you discover?

9

POST-TRAUMATIC STRESS DISORDER
IN AN ADOLESCENT:
THE CASE OF ZOE M

EVERYONE AGREED: Zoe was drop-dead gorgeous. Her long blond hair, luminous blue eyes, perfect teeth in a perfect smile, and willowy body involuntarily turned the heads of both men and women in school, on the street, and in the mall. It was hard to believe that this stunning sixteen-year-old was the same girl who had been called "rat-face" in elementary school.

Mr. M, an executive at a Fortune 500 company, and Mrs. M, a homemaker and artist, had brought their daughter for help in coping with a bizarre and frightening experience that had occurred a few months earlier. To explain the incident, they had to go back a ways. Zoe had been a shy and timid but loving youngster. She had had some difficulty managing the transition to school when she was five, complaining each morning for the first several weeks that she had a stomachache and needed to stay home. Mrs. M, upon the advice of Zoe's pediatrician, remained firm about sending Zoe to school anyway, and the episodes passed. Zoe was a good student, a talented violinist in the school orchestra, and a favorite of most of the teachers. She had several good friends throughout elementary school, which helped to balance the suffering she endured at the hands of others of her peers who seemed to take particular delight in teasing her until she cried—which didn't take long.

Zoe's junior high career had been even more turbulent, however. She seemed moody and unhappy a lot of the time. Her friends were discovering boys but Zoe didn't quite know how to flirt, and her awkward attempts often fell flat. By ninth grade, she had fallen in with a crowd of bright misfits. Her parents reported that these youngsters smoked marijuana, cut school frequently, and spent hours each evening discussing "philosophy" in online chat rooms. Mr. and Mrs. M had tried to tell Zoe that these youngsters were not on the right track, but she always defended them vociferously, and the level of conflict in the household gradually escalated.

One young man, in particular, worried Zoe's parents. He was a self-declared Satanist who dressed in black and had various Satanic symbols tattooed on his body. He had dropped out of school altogether at the age of sixteen and was working part time in an auto body shop, much to the chagrin of his mother, a divorced attorney. Mrs. M described him as so "creepy" that she finally refused to allow him in her home, despite Zoe's pleas and rages.

One night, a few months back, just about bedtime, this young man came to the door and spoke to Zoe for a few minutes. Zoe told her parents that he had decided to hitchhike cross-country and wanted her to come with him. Despite his agitated pleadings, she had refused, she proudly told them. "See," she had said to them, "I have better judgment than you think."

Little did she know how right she was, for later that night this youngster stabbed his mother eighteen times with a kitchen knife, stole her money and her car, and left her bleeding to death in the bedroom of his family home. He had left a message in her blood on the bedroom mirror. It said "hate = love."

The next several weeks had been a horror show for Zoe and her family. Local police and the FBI had interviewed Zoe numerous times, as she had been the last person her friend had contacted before the crime. They showed her pictures of the murder scene in order to impress upon her the seriousness of the situation, lest she be protecting him in some way. At school she was a pariah. Her presence provoked muted whispers and marked avoidance. Several students had taken to making the sign of the cross when they passed her in the hall. When this didn't let up after a month, Mr. and Mrs. M decided to enroll Zoe in a private school in a neighboring city where her association with this heinous crime could be kept quiet.

Zoe had made the transition to the new school surprisingly well. She joined the orchestra, where she happened to make friends with one of the school's most popular girls. She stayed away from the marginal youngsters and worked hard at her studies.

However, she had not escaped unscathed. Recently, she had become more and more afraid of being alone. At first, she had felt uncomfortable in her room at night while trying to fall asleep. She kept picturing her friend's face at her door and his mother's bloody body in the bed.

No matter how she tried to avoid it, the image kept popping back into her head, causing her heart to beat so hard she thought she was dying. She tried a night light, which helped some, but she could only sleep well if her door were open and the light in the hall were left on. Gradually, she found herself unable to remain at home alone without discomfort. The after-school hours were torturous, and she tried to spend each afternoon at a friend's house until her parents were home. She had difficulty walking outdoors at night. She could no longer walk the family dog. Even with friends, if a stranger approached them unexpectedly, her heart would pound and she would feel lightheaded. Since the scary images in her mind could be stimulated by an expanding set of cues, she avoided movies or television shows that had any violence in them. Her parents reported that, despite her academic and social success at the new school, she was becoming moodier and moodier, irritable over nothing and tearful at the drop of a hat. They, themselves, were furious at her for bringing this trouble into their family and were fed up with her emotionality. They wanted things back to normal.

Zoe's therapy took about seven months. At first, she and her therapist met weekly, and Zoe had the opportunity to describe, in detail, her feelings about her experience. The therapist listened carefully and validated each of the feelings that Zoe expressed. Zoe grieved the loss of the safe world she had known as a child and began to accept that terrible things did indeed happen from time to time. Together they worked to identify and reduce the overgeneralizations that had entered Zoe's thinking after the trauma: "Now I can *never* be safe again"; "when it gets dark, something terrible is *certain* to happen"; "*all* strangers are dangerous."

The therapist also taught Zoe some strategies designed to counteract the physical symptoms of anxiety. One of these was "square breathing." It involved inhaling to a count of three, holding the breath for a count of three, exhaling for a count of three, and pausing for a count of three before inhaling again. This was effective in preventing Zoe from hyperventilating when something startled or frightened her. Through repeatedly pairing her square breathing with the intrusive visual images that frightened her, Zoe was able to gain some control over the amount of anxiety these images induced.

Zoe also talked with her therapist about the shame and embarrassment her association with the incident had caused her and her family. She felt stupid and even tainted with evil. Her therapist helped her understand why she had been vulnerable to the influence of this particular peer group and reminded her of the strength she had shown in cooperating with the police and in returning to a more pro-social stance. Together they came to the inevitable conclusion that mistakes are a part of growing up.

A few family sessions were interspersed throughout the therapy. With the therapist's guidance, Zoe's parents expressed how frightened they had been for her. Zoe's father said, "It's like when a child runs into the road. When you get them back, you don't know whether to hug them or spank them. We were angry at Zoe for scaring us so badly." The therapist educated them about the symptoms of post-traumatic stress disorder, which helped them to adopt a more support-ive and less punitive stance.

By therapy's end, Zoe was much improved. She was less moody and more like her old self. She was still prone to sudden bouts of anxiety and occasional intrusive thoughts or visual images, but she had learned how to manage them more successfully so that they didn't last very long or interfere with her activities as much as they had previously. She thought of herself as a survivor, as someone who could master an unexpected and difficult situation. Her parents had come to a greater understanding of what she had gone through and had developed an admiration for her fortitude. At follow-up, one year later, she appeared to be doing well.

Thinking about the Case

Unlike phobias or adjustment disorders, which are precipitated by common objects or events, post-traumatic stress disorders (PTSDs) occur in response to exceptional stressors, beyond the usual range of human suffering. Battlefield experiences, concentration camp incarcer-ation, rape, mugging, natural disaster (earthquake, flood, or fire), witnessing a bloody accident—events like these in which the individual is exposed to some sort of serious threat to self or others can all produce debilitating and long-lasting psychological and physiological symptoms.

Three sets of symptoms define PTSD: (1) persistent reexperience of the trauma and the feelings associated with it in dreams, images, flashbacks, thoughts, or perceptions, (2) avoidance of stimuli that are associated with the trauma and a general numbing of responsiveness, and (3) persistent symptoms of increased anxiety and arousal, such as difficulty sleeping, exaggerated startle reaction, irritability, bursts of anger, and difficulty concentrating. Guilt about having survived the trauma when others did not or about how one behaved during the traumatic event is also common. Individuals with PTSD often have problems maintaining relationships due to irritability and difficulties developing emotional attachments. Their work or school performance may be impaired by difficulties concentrating, reduced motivation, and outbursts of anger. They are at increased risk for episodes of depression and may attempt to medicate their anxiety with alcohol and drugs.

Wars and natural disasters have afforded a great deal of opportunity to study the natural course of PTSD. In general, the more extensive, prolonged, and horrific the exposure to trauma, the more severe and persistent the symptoms. For example, almost all survivors of Nazi concentration camps were troubled with persistent anxiety twenty years after they were freed from the camps. A majority had anxiety dreams and nightmares, while many also suffered daytime fears that something terrible would happen to their loved ones whenever they were out of sight. Studies of rape victims indicate that a substantial minority experience post-traumatic symptoms for decades following the incident.

Not all individuals who are exposed to a particular trauma will develop PTSD. Who is at risk? Of particular interest are studies of resiliency in children: What allows the majority of children who suffer traumas like floods and earthquakes to recover so well? What distinguishes them from the children who develop PTSD symptoms? Are there early intervention or prevention techniques that might instill resiliency in vulnerable children?

Studies suggest that those with the highest levels of mental health prior to the trauma have the best prognosis, reinforcing once again the old adage "the best predictor of future behavior is past behavior." Researchers have hypothesized that PTSD may even have a heritable component that interacts with the severity of trauma in predicting outcome. For children, the adequacy of their parents' own coping and ability to provide support for the youngsters is a likely factor in prevention of sustained symptomatology.

Given the severity of dysfunction that often accompanies PTSD, and the grave prognosis for at least a substantial percentage of sufferers, finding treatments that work is critical. While medications are sometimes helpful in ameliorating some of the symptoms of PTSD, they never result in a cure. Psychotherapy is always necessary. It would appear that telling about the trauma to a sympathetic and affirming listener has some curative power, although, interestingly, the listener may experience nightmares, fears, increased anxiety, or depression in this process. There is some evidence that talking about the trauma in a group setting with others who have experienced similar life events has additional value.

Behavioral methods that are used to treat phobias have been applied to PTSD with some success. Prolonged exposure therapy in which the individual is repeatedly exposed to the feared stimulus, relaxation techniques, and cognitive restructuring like Zoe experienced have all been shown to be helpful.

The Developmental Perspective

Trauma can occur at any stage of an individual's life. What differs is the person's ability to master the trauma. This can depend, at least in part, on the level of cognitive and emotional development attained prior to the traumatic incident. For example, young children who have been traumatized have few verbal and cognitive skills with which to "understand" what happened to them. They tend to respond by regressing to earlier stages of development, becoming clingy, incontinent, or mute, for example. They also tend to use play to reinact or work through the trauma. Therapists can harness this natural propensity by incorporating drawing or playing with dolls or figurines into the therapy process.

The effects of trauma can persist, reappear, or even appear for the first time years after the traumatic event occurred. For example, clinicians observe that traumatized adolescents appear less able to contain anger and engage in self-destructive behaviors more often than their peers. They appear to be at greater risk for drug and alcohol problems, self-mutilative behavior, promiscuity, and conflictful relationships. This is true even if the trauma occurred some years before and appeared to have little effect on the youngster at the time. This appears to be so because trauma can damage the individual's ability to regulate emotions and relate to others, two skills that are highly taxed in adolescence.

Another example can be found in young women whose sexual trauma in childhood can be reactivated by an adult sexual relationship or by the birth of a child. Many of these women who appear virtually asymptomatic for years can develop acute post-traumatic symptoms in a situation that provokes memories of the trauma.

In general, the more history of positive emotional development and mastery of life problems the individual has when the trauma occurs, the better. It has even been hypothesized that some individuals are virtually inoculated against the effects of trauma by a childhood and adolescence marked by superior problem-solving skills and a strong emotional foundation.

Questions to Consider

1. What aspects of Zoe's history are good prognostic signs? What aspects are poor ones? Would you have predicted that she would recover fairly well? Why or why not?

2. Have you or a close friend or family member ever had symptoms of post-traumatic stress disorder? Which ones? How long did they last? What aspects of the person's environment supported or hindered recovery? What aspects of the person's own personality or coping skills supported or hindered recovery?

3. It is generally thought that the effects of man-made trauma like war or abuse situations are worse than the effects of natural disasters like fire or flood. Why do you think this might be so?

4. Suppose parents wanted to raise a resilient child who could withstand traumatic events without developing prolonged symptoms. How might they go about doing so? How much of the child's future resiliency do you think would be under the parent's influence?

10

POST-TRAUMATIC STRESS DISORDER
IN A YOUNGER CHILD:
THE CASE OF LUIS P

MRS. P WAS DESPERATE to get help for Luis, her younger and favorite child. So great was her concern that she violated her family's long-standing prohibition against telling outsiders their problems by seeking assistance from the community mental health center located within walking distance of her apartment. The intake worker at the center wisely assigned a bilingual therapist to work with Luis so that his mother would not have to struggle to communicate.

In the interview, little eight-year-old Luis sat quietly, head bowed, while his mother related her concerns. Luis was having serious problems at home and at school. Despite having an above-average I.Q., he was having trouble completing his homework. His teacher said that he was inattentive at school and seemed sad and moody. At home, he seemed not so much sad as angry. He was argumentative and irritable with his mother. Worse yet, he was aggressive with his ten-year-old sister who was, nonetheless, unfailingly loving and protective toward him. For no apparent reason he would scream at her, and a few days before the interview he had hit her with a baseball bat. After these rages he seemed genuinely remorseful, apologizing over and over and asking repeatedly whether his sister and mother still loved him. At these times he clung to them, wrapping his arms around their legs or holding on to their clothes until he was reassured that they did indeed still love him.

Mrs. P also mentioned that Luis seemed unable to relax. He startled easily and complained of frequent nightmares. Often he could not sleep unless she let him climb into bed with her, and she noticed that he talked in his sleep many nights. He had recently reverted to sucking on his fingers, a self-soothing behavior that he had given up when he began kindergarten. At other times, though, he seemed to be in a fog, not hearing what was said to him or unable to follow the plot of his favorite television show.

The therapist decided to split sessions, seeing Luis for the first half and his mother for the second half. With Luis, she played the "Talking, Feeling, and Doing Game," a board game that creates opportunities for children to talk about their feelings about various life situations. With Mrs. P, she explored some of the family's recent history for clues about Luis's problems. The full picture emerged slowly, over the course of eight sessions.

Luis's biological father had been an abusive alcoholic who had beaten his wife and both of the children. He had left Mrs. P for another woman when Luis was four. Visits with Mr. P were inconsistent and, apparently, terrifying. When Luis's sister told her mother that Luis had been locked in a closet for several hours by Mr. P as a punishment for misbehaving, the visits were abruptly stopped. But the worst was yet to come.

After Mr. and Mrs. P split up, Mrs. P soon met and moved the family in with another man, Mr. A. While he, too, had a drinking problem like Mr. P, he was different in that he didn't get angry when he was drunk. Rather, he became sad and morose, often crying himself to sleep at night after a binge. Mr. A loved children and behaved like a father to Luis and his sister. Over the next year and a half, both children became quite close to him. However, their relationship with him ended tragically when Mr. A put a gun to his head one evening when only the children were home and blew his brains out.

Mrs. P was bereft. She spent months in the house, being taken care of by her mother and sisters. Some days she was too weighed down by grief to even get out of bed. The children fended for themselves as best they could, with the help of their grandmother and aunts. She had recovered slowly, she said, and as she did so, she noticed Luis's problems more and more. She couldn't say whether he was actually getting worse or, instead, her ability to attend to his problems was improving.

Meanwhile, Luis was revealing more about himself as well. Not surprisingly, his dreams were about Mr. A's suicide. Over and over he dreamed that Mr. A's head exploded while he tried in vain to get to Mr. A before the gun went off. In the dream he would try to scream but couldn't. He would try to move but couldn't. He could only watch, terrified, as the horrific event repeated itself.

Luis told the counselor that he hated his life and wanted to die.

Nothing he did gave him any pleasure. He was mad all the time. He had tried to run away from home but didn't know where to go. He wanted to be with Mr. A, with whom he envisioned a happy life in heaven.

Alarmed by the extent of Luis's depression, the counselor recommended regular psychotherapy and a psychiatric evaluation to see whether medication might be helpful. Mrs. P's family was dead set against "giving pills to a baby," so Mrs. P refused the psychiatric evaluation. She did allow Luis to continue in therapy, however, where he was able to use drawing, painting, dolls, and talking to express his feelings about Mr. A's suicide and the multiple losses he had experienced. Mrs. P received counseling about how to help Luis express feelings appropriately at home, and she was given an opportunity to discuss her own losses and her fears of coping with life without a man to help her. Together Mrs. P and the therapist came up with the idea of asking one of Luis's uncles to take a special interest in Luis. They chose her oldest sister's husband, who had been in the family for over fifteen years and seemed both stable and kind. This uncle was flattered by Mrs. P's request and took his "godfather" duties quite seriously.

Over the course of the next several months Luis's nightmares, clinging, inattention, and irritability began to improve. However, by this time, Mrs. P had begun dating another man with whom she moved to the other side of the city. Plans were made to transfer Luis's care to another mental health center, but the intake appointment was not kept and the family was lost to follow-up.

Thinking about the Case

Luis showed each of the symptoms of post-traumatic stress disorder (PTSD), described in the discussion of Zoe M's case (Case 9). He reexperienced the trauma in dreams, had a numbing of responsiveness ("in a fog"), and showed numerous symptoms of anxiety and arousal. However, PTSD often co-occurs with other psychiatric diagnoses. Luis also had symptoms of clinical depression: inability to experience pleasure, depressed mood, decreased concentration, irritability, and thoughts of death. In an ideal treatment plan, both problems would have been addressed.

Luis's case illustrates clearly how problems of parents can contribute to problems experienced by children. Luis's mother was a dependent woman who could not stay long without a man in her life. Therefore, Luis was subjected to a series of attachments and losses throughout his childhood. This predisposed him not only to depression but also to problems with attachment, problems that might reappear later in life when he tried to establish adult relationships. In choosing the first man rather than the best man to attach herself to after her children's father left, Mrs. P exposed Luis and his sister to a poor role model and to possible danger. In addition, her consuming grief prevented her from attending to the needs of her children immediately after Mr. A's suicide. Had she been more emotionally available, she might have been able to mitigate somewhat the effects of the trauma and loss Luis and his sister suffered. Fully successful treatment of Luis would likely have involved psychotherapy for his mother as well.

This case also shows how cultural and family-system factors can affect the course of therapy. Mrs. P was part of a large, supportive extended family who could be expected to influence the therapy process for good or for ill. The opinions of Mrs. P's relatives influenced her cooperation with therapy recommendations. A savvy counselor might have thought to enlist Mrs. P's mother as an ally as therapy progressed by inviting her into sessions and by seeking her advice along the way. However, identifying an uncle as "godfather" to Luis was a creative way to enlist the support of the family in caring for Luis's needs.

The Developmental Perspective

Note the differences between Luis's and Zoe's responses to trauma, several of which are related to their developmental stages. Where Luis regressed to earlier coping strategies, including clinging and sucking his fingers, Zoe, whose problem-solving skills were more advanced, attempted to master her fears by using a night light and spending time with friends. In addition, Zoe was able to voice her fears and knew where they came from. Therefore, she was able to encapsulate her problem to some extent and maintain her superior school and social performance. Typical of younger children who are less able to conceptualize why they feel bad or to label the feelings accurately, Luis's deficits were more diffuse, affecting all areas of functioning. Notice also that while Luis had thoughts of death, he was unable to organize and carry out a set of behaviors that would allow him to act on these thoughts. In fact, he was too young even to figure out how to run away successfully. Older youngsters who experience these wishes are at greater risk of acting on them.

Therapy took these youngsters' development into account. Zoe's therapy was conversational and educational in nature. She identified her feelings and corrected distortions in her thinking. She learned strategies for mastering anxiety. Luis's therapy utilized natural play situations and expressive media: board games, dolls, drawing, and painting. Through these, he essentially acted out his feelings in the safe environment of the therapy room.

In addition, Luis's therapy involved his mother as a matter of necessity and might profitably have involved other important people in his life. Zoe, on the other hand, was more independent and was able to problem-solve about the social aspects of her troubles. Therapy with younger children always involves parents, who are the main agents of modifying the child's environment, whereas adolescents can often modify their own environments. Thus, involvement of parents in treatment is optional and depends on the specifics of the case.

Questions to Consider

1. How might the loss of the therapist affect Luis? Should consideration of this eventuality influence the type of treatment proposed? How might the effects of this loss be mitigated?

2. What are some possible reasons that Mrs. P failed to keep her appointment with the new therapist at the new clinic? What steps might have been taken to avert this failure?

3. What sorts of problems in adulthood might arise for a youngster like Luis who is subjected to a series of his mother's live-in boyfriends? Explain in developmental terms why these problems might arise.

11

UNDIFFERENTIATED SOMATOFORM
DISORDER: THE CASE OF ALINE N

ALINE WAS A fragile-looking, slightly built eleven-year-old girl with scraggly blond hair that hung loose to her shoulders. A few months previously, she had begun fifth grade at the local public school after having gone to parochial school for kindergarten through fourth grade. While she had never been a particularly good student, she had always been a well-behaved and compliant child, shy almost to the point of being withdrawn. Now, however, she appeared to be increasingly distressed. She left class often to visit the nurse. She complained of headaches and chills—and, indeed, looked pale and ill. Other times, she complained of feeling nauseated and of vomiting. She had sore throats and upset stomachs. She felt faint, had trouble breathing, appeared to be hyperventilating. While she rarely failed to get to school, thanks to the ministrations of a strict grandmother, she was spending less and less time in the classroom. Numerous visits to her pediatrician failed to reveal organic reasons for her symptoms. Finally, after months of feeling ill and miserable, Aline was referred to a psychotherapist for evaluation and treatment.

Aline's family situation was somewhat atypical. Her father was a tall, handsome, rugged police officer. He was a strict, no-nonsense parent. He had known Aline's mother since she had moved in with his family years ago when they were both teenagers. Apparently one of her parents had had a bout of major mental illness and the other had been unable to parent her, so she had moved in with Mr. N's parents, who had been friends of the family. Mr. and Mrs. N married when they were in their early twenties.

Mrs. N was, by reputation, not a very good caregiver. Reports from the parochial school indicated that the children often appeared dirty and hungry when they arrived in the mornings. Still, Aline felt closer to her mother, than to her father. Interestingly, she looked like her mother, who was also fragile and delicately built.

After several years of marital conflict, Mrs. N had left the family about a year before Aline entered therapy. Aline had been devastated by her mother's leaving and furious at her father. She threatened to go live with her mother, but Mrs. N, by this time engaged to another man, was not eager to have her. Mr. N had tried for about half a year to woo his wife back home and had finally made her a generous financial settlement in order to protect his custody of the children.

Aline had a younger brother who was quite different from her. Rugged rather than frail, well adjusted with lots of friends, Robert appeared to take his mother's leaving fairly calmly.

Living only two doors away and functioning virtually as a surrogate parent was Aline's paternal grandmother. She had helped to raise Mrs. N but had never felt her to be emotionally stable and had been privately dismayed when Mr. N had decided to marry her. Now Mr. N's mother found herself intimately involved in raising her grandchildren, despite the fact that her own health was failing. She had diabetes and high blood pressure and had recently been diagnosed with osteoarthritis that was affecting both of her hips.

While Aline had been shy but apparently contented in parochial school, in the public school her lack of social skills began to cause her substantial torment. The teacher reported that she kept trying to make friends but seemed to bungle each attempt. Other children found her too pushy or silly or were made anxious by her social awkwardness. They called her "nurse's baby" because she seemed always to be ill and asking to be excused from class. In addition, she seemed hypersensitive and took offense to every perceived slight, both real and imagined. Her complaints of being teased by peers were as likely to be exaggerated as accurate. Not surprisingly, the more she complained that other children teased and hurt her, the less they wanted to have anything to do with her.

The therapist hypothesized that some of Aline's symptoms were likely due to unresolved feelings about her family problems. However, Aline steadfastly refused to talk about them realistically. Instead, she was elated one week because her mother was going to get married and she was going to be in the wedding party and totally deflated the next when wedding plans were postponed. She didn't seem able to develop a stable, realistic image of Mrs. N, but saw her as all good and giving or totally disappointing and worthless.

After Aline had been in therapy for some weeks, impressed by the depth of Aline's misery her therapist requested a psychiatric consultation. The psychiatrist prescribed an antidepressant medication. Within ten days of beginning this treatment, Aline's teacher reported that Aline had become giddy, loud, silly, and uncharacteristically disruptive in class. The medication was decreased and ultimately discontinued, without having produced any benefit.

In the meantime, Aline entered a social skills training group that met on a weekly basis. In this group she practiced listening to other children, understanding their feelings, giving compliments, and making conversation. Perhaps as a result of her increasing ability to consider another's viewpoint, she managed to make one friend, a youngster whose own pain engendered a supportive, empathic response from Aline. Her ability to be helpful to this friend increased her self-esteem and gave her the courage to try to engage other classmates.

At the same time, the therapist worked with Mr. N to help him understand Aline's needs better. She empathized with Mr. N about how hard it was to be both father and mother to the children and gave him an opportunity to talk about his own pain and insecurities. He even talked about how much Aline reminded him of his ex-wife and how difficult it was to treat her in a warm, supportive way.

The therapist also noticed that both Mr. N and his mother had a natural preference for Aline's brother. She hypothesized that perhaps Aline's physical complaints got her some attention, particularly from her father, who routinely pampered her with special foods and activities when she was ill. The therapist counseled both Mr. N and his mother to respond to Aline's physical complaints in a more matter-of-fact fashion. In addition, they worked on overcoming their preference for Aline's brother and found in her traits to admire and enjoy.

Mr. N's mother was a resource in the therapy process, as she had been a resource in the children's lives. She quickly acknowledged that her own anger at her daughter-in-law had been inappropriately communicated to the children and promised to stop "badmouthing" Mrs. N to Aline. She accepted and began to actively support Aline's need to love her mother, which in turn helped Aline become more realistic about Mrs. N, since she no longer felt she had to defend her constantly.

Over the school year, Aline gradually improved, although not without some setbacks. For example, she incurred a suspension for taking a knife to school (one of her father's that she was taking to show her friend) and accused (it appeared falsely) her mother's current boyfriend of sexually molesting her. Still, her physical complaints dropped markedly and she no longer seemed to be trying to escape the classroom situation. She developed a few tentative friendships and complained less of being teased. The quality of her academic work increased and she seemed less sensitive, moody, and miserable. Her family and teacher felt that significant change had been achieved.

Thinking about the Case

It is not uncommon for youngsters to voice recurrent or persistent physical complaints for which no organic cause can be found. The diagnostic criteria for the somatoform disorders were established for adults and are applied to children because of a lack of child-specific research and a developmentally appropriate alternative. For example, the diagnosis of somatization disorder, which is defined by a long history of multiple physical complaints, requires the presence of at least one sexual symptom. Therefore, it is virtually never diagnosed in preadolescent youngsters like Aline. Instead, she is diagnosed as having undifferentiated somatoform disorder, a residual category for individuals who have multiple physical complaints but do not meet the strict criteria for somatization disorder. The prevalence rate for somatizing disorders in adults is estimated at somewhere around 10 percent, with more females being diagnosed than males. The prevalence rate for youngsters is unknown, although onset is typically during adolescence.

This case illustrates nicely the interweaving of constitutional, psychological, and social factors that often contribute to the development of maladjustment. Aline clearly had a shy and interpersonally sensitive temperament that precipitated problems with peers, particularly when combined with her social awkwardness. She also had a family history of mental illness on her mother's side, which may have played a role as well: Anxiety, depression, and other psychiatric symptoms have been found to be overrepresented in families of somatizing children.

There is evidence that Aline suffered from some amount of emotional, and perhaps physical, neglect at various points in her childhood. She and her brother were poorly dressed and groomed by their mother before she left the family. Mrs. N's ongoing connection to the children after the separation seemed tenuous and marked by disappointments. Mr. N appeared to have difficulty making emotional connections, and Aline's grandmother was strict and preoccupied with her own physical problems. Both her father and grandmother preferred her brother to Aline. Empirical work does suggest that emotional neglect, particularly when followed by childhood illness, may lead to somatizing disorders.

Modeling and secondary reinforcement may also have played a role in the genesis of Aline's physical complaints. Research suggests that the presence of family members with chronic physical illness may be associated with increased somatic symptoms in children. Aline's grandmother had multiple physical problems that required discussion and treatment and Mr. N responded, uncharacteristically, to Aline's physical complaints. These same complaints also served to remove her from the stressful peer environment in school and garner her the attention of the school nurse, who may have been a caregiving stand-in for both mother and grandmother.

Some experts hypothesize that somatizing disorders occur in individuals who repress feelings and conflicts. While Aline was able to express her dismay at how she was treated by peers, it is possible that feelings of anger, hurt, and abandonment generated by the behavior of family members were less accessible to her awareness, thus requring expression indirectly through physical symptoms.

Treatment of somatizing disorders needs to address both the psychological conflicts or issues that may be represented through the symptoms and the behavioral components of secondary gain. Parents need to be counseled not to inadvertently reinforce "symptom talk" or to allow symptoms to provide an escape route from stressful situations. However, even with treatment, these disorders tend to be persistent through life, often following a chronic fluctuating course.

The Developmental Perspective

Somatic and pain symptoms appear to follow a developmental sequence. Initially, they tend to be monosymptomatic. In younger children, recurrent abdominal pain followed by headaches appears to be most common. Limb pain, aching muscles, fatigue, and neurological symptoms increase with age.

It is thought that prepubertal children are more likely to experience emotional distress as somatic sensations because they lack the experience and vocabulary to accurately distinguish these states. Therefore, an adolescent or adult might say "I'm anxious," whereas a youngster might say "My stomach is jittery." Some youngsters, probably for complex and multifaceted reasons, may fail to progress in their ability to identify emotional states and instead remain overreactive to internal, physiological cues into adulthood. Indeed, a history of undifferentiated somatoform disorder in youngsters is associated with a diagnosis of somatization disorder in adulthood.

Questions to Consider

1. How would you account for the differences in adjustment between Aline and her brother? What light does your account shed (if any) on the nature-nurture controversy?

2. Undifferentiated somatoform disorder occurs most commonly in women of low socioeconomic status. Why might this be so?

3. Somatization disorder appears to occur more often in conjunction with personality disorders than with other Axis I disorders. Why might this be so?

4. It has been reported that somatization disorder is frequently associated with sexual abuse in childhood. Why might this be so?

5. Have you ever had unexplained somatic symptoms? What hypotheses can you develop about their possible psychological causes?

PART THREE

Mood Disorders

———◄O►———

Everyone has felt blue, lonely, or disheartened from time to time. When these feelings are accompanied by physical changes like sleep disturbance and weight loss, or behavioral changes like social withdrawal or poor hygiene, or cognitive changes like decreased concentration and memory, depression may be diagnosed. On the other end of the spectrum, extreme joy, euphoria, and accelerated activity can suggest a clinical condition we call mania. Like the other psychological disorders, mood disorders vary in intensity, duration, and treatability. And, like other disorders, they are best understood within a biopsychosocial framework.

Mood disorders are common in children as well as adults. While low mood is universally observed across the developmental spectrum, depression in younger children is more reactive to environmental changes and includes fewer of the cognitive distortions commonly observed in older depressed youngsters. In all cases, treatment generally includes a combination of biological, psychological, and social interventions.

In this section, we include four cases. The first concerns a ten-year-old girl who experiences a series of losses and develops a fairly serious depression. The second presents an example of bipolar disorder; a boy develops this disorder during adolescence which is the typical age of onset. In the third case, a sixteen-year-old girl exhibits a chronic form of depression called dysthymia, and in the fourth, a little boy reacts to the separation of his parents. We have included both acute and chronic forms of depression, as well as depression across the developmental spectrum, so that we can consider their differences and commonalities.

12

MAJOR DEPRESSION:
THE CASE OF ONOLEE B

ONOLEE DIDN'T CRY at her mother's funeral. Sandwiched between her rigidly erect father and her sobbing grandmother, the slightly built African-American ten-year-old girl stared vacantly ahead as the minister read the eulogy. Her four-year-old brother sat on their grandmother's lap, but she was a big girl and had to sit quietly and not make trouble. After the funeral, at her grandmother's house where all the family had gathered, Onolee suffered through the hugs and condolences of her aunts, uncles, and cousins. Through it all, she was puzzled by how little emotion she felt; it was as if she had turned into a robot, going through the motions but not really there.

Onolee seemed to be doing fairly well over the next few months. The family moved in with Mr. B's mother, so somebody would be around to take care of Onolee and her brother while her father worked. Onolee enjoyed both of her grandmothers, but this one particularly lavished both children with extra amounts of love and attention to make up for the loss of their mother. She took them to the park after school and, on rainy days, baked cookies or a pie, often letting Onolee help. Onolee's father was working long hours; he seemed tired and irritable a lot of the time. Onolee learned not to bother him, except on Sundays, when he took them all to church and then out to lunch. On Sundays, he was more himself. He didn't laugh much, but at least he listened while Onolee told him about her week.

At school, Onolee remained a quiet and obedient child who was well liked by her fourth-grade teacher and by most of the other children in her class. She was an average student, and she played trumpet in the elementary school band. For a while, after her mother died, she seemed somewhat listless, but within a few weeks her functioning returned to its normal level.

After about eight months, Mr. B met and began to date a woman from the neighborhood. This woman, Fran, was a single mother with two children of her own. She was nice to Onolee when she saw her, but often she and Onolee's dad went off on their own. Fran began attending church and Sunday lunch with the family each week, and finally, after about six months, Mr. B announced that he and the children would be moving in with her. Onolee didn't protest her father's decision, despite her fervent wish that they would all stay where they were. She knew her father would never listen to her—it would only make him mad. Anyway, he seemed really happy when he was with Fran, and Onolee wanted very much for her father to be happy after such a long time of sadness.

The move seemed to go reasonably well. Onolee had to share a room with Fran's eight-year-old daughter, Issie. She tried to think of herself as Issie's older sister as her father had requested and to be patient when Issie rooted through her things and wore her clothes. She tried not to be bothered by the level of disorder in their new home. After all, there were twice as many children and twice as much to do. As the oldest, she was expected to help out as much as possible by setting the table, sorting the laundry, and vacuuming one room a day. All of this she did, if not willingly, at least cooperatively. Church and lunch with her grandmother remained an inviolable Sunday ritual.

Over the next several months, Onolee's teacher noticed a perceptible change in her behavior. She seemed even quieter than normal and uncharacteristically prone to outbursts of temper or tears if one of the other children bumped her or playfully teased her. It looked as if she wasn't getting enough rest: She had circles under her eyes and she had no energy. Her concentration seemed to be impaired and she began to show up at school with homework sloppy, incomplete, or not even attempted. Onolee's band teacher corroborated her homeroom teacher's report; Onolee was having trouble learning the new pieces and the band steps. Previously, she had been one of the best, most enthusiastic band members. One day, Onolee's teacher assigned an essay called "My Deepest Wish." She was so frightened by Onolee's essay that she decided to call Mr. B. Onolee had written that her deepest wish was to be with her mother in heaven.

Mr. B was unable to come to the school meeting because he had to work, but Onolee's grandmother came in his stead. She had spoken with her son and with Fran to get their impressions and reported that they, too, had some concerns. Onolee had seemed irritable at home, too. Her appetite and her energy level had diminished in recent weeks.

She appeared to be losing weight. They had also reported that Onolee was always apologizing to everybody for any little thing. When she had found out that her teacher was concerned about her, she had burst into tears, apologizing to her father for being a problem and promising that she would do better. He had reassured her that he wasn't mad, just worried, but it hadn't seemed to help; she had appeared inconsolable.

At the teacher's suggestion, Mr. B took Onolee to the local community mental health center for an evaluation. A psychologist talked with Onolee and had her draw a few pictures and answer several written questions. He also spoke with Onolee's father and grandmother as well as with Fran and Onolee's teacher to get everybody's perspective on the problem.

After gathering as much information as he could, the psychologist met with Mr. B, his mother, and Fran to discuss treatment possibilities. He told them that Onolee had "major depression," which could usually be treated quite successfully. He explained that Onolee had suffered several losses that had overwhelmed her capacity to cope. First, in addition to losing her mother, Onolee had lost some of the closeness in her relationship with her grandmother when her father had moved them in with Fran. Second, she had lost some access to her father, first because of his own private grieving and later because of his involvement with Fran. Third, she had lost some privacy and autonomy in having to adjust to stepsiblings and in sharing a bedroom. Since she was a shy and obedient child, she was unlikely to voice her concerns in a way that anybody could hear. While the new living situation might very well, in the long run, be wonderful for Onolee, it took some getting used to in the short run.

The psychologist suggested that Onolee be treated with an antidepressant medication and psychotherapy. He also suggested some family counseling sessions to help Onolee learn to be a bit more open in expressing her needs and to help the whole family adjust to the myriad changes they had encountered recently. While Mr. B generally agreed with the psychologist's ideas about what was causing Onolee's "depression," he was adamantly opposed to medication treatment. He didn't want to "mess with Onolee's brain," and, besides, he had heard on television about how those medicines were overprescribed. He did agree, however, to having Onolee meet with the psychologist regularly. He knew that she had had a rough year, and he could sense that she was not herself and felt that she would benefit if she had someone to talk to who understood how to help her. He knew, too, that, as much as he wanted to help his daughter, he hadn't a clue how to begin. He also agreed to family sessions, provided that they were held in the evening so that he didn't have to miss work, and to this the psychologist readily agreed.

In Onolee's weekly meetings with the psychologist, sometimes they talked, sometimes they drew pictures and talked about them, sometimes they played a board game called the "Talking, Feeling, and Doing Game." Once she began to feel comfortable in the therapy room, Onolee talked often about her mother. She talked about how bad she felt for not appreciating her mother enough when she was alive, for being angry at her father for withdrawing, for resenting Fran and her children. The therapist responded to each of these concerns by listening and gently letting Onolee know that most children had similar feelings from time to time.

The therapist had several goals for the family meetings. The first was to open some lines of communication between Onolee and her dad, to give Onolee a greater sense of safety in expressing her feelings verbally to her father. He hoped that her father might respond supportively to some of her concerns so that she would experience a greater sense of control in her life. The second was to help her realize that she was not the only one having a rough time. The transition had been hard for everyone, including Fran and her children, and each person had responded in his or her own unique way. He felt that this would help Onolee feel less guilty about her feelings. The third was to clarify the roles in the new family—for example, who would set and enforce the rules for Onolee, her father or Fran or both?

Prior to the first family meeting, the psychologist had a private session with Mr. B and Fran in which he suggested that listening to Onolee was the best gift her father could give her; he didn't have to do anything in particular in the sessions to help her feel better except let her know that it was safe to tell him what bothered her. The therapist also suggested that Onolee's problem might be helped if she could feel some measure of control of her life. He left it to Mr. B and Fran to figure out how this might be accomplished. The therapist acknowledged Mr. B's highly developed sense of responsibility for his daughter's welfare, his willingness to work long hours to support her, his consistency in providing the important Sunday family days, and his thoughtfulness in considering the treatment plan. The psychologist acknowledged how difficult it was for fathers to engage in "all this talking" and complimented Mr. B for his willingness to participate in therapy for his daughter's sake. He thanked Fran as well for caring enough about Onolee and her father to attend.

In the family meetings, which included Fran, her two children, and

Mr. B's mother, the therapist encouraged each member to talk about how he or she had experienced the loss of Onolee's mother and about how the families were doing together. Onolee was amazed that her father also felt grief and uncertainty sometimes. He had seemed to her to feel nothing at all. They also talked about household rules, who had what chores, what punishments could be expected for misbehavior. Hesitantly, Onolee expressed her sadness at not seeing her other grand-mother and her mother's family more often. In response, Mr. B arranged for her to do so. Onolee expressed surprise that her father wasn't angry at her for "wanting to spend time away from you-all." Mr. B told her that he knew that she had more than enough love to go around and that he was happy to help her spend time with the other people she loved. He also began to spend some time each evening going over her homework with her and asking about her day. Fran had the idea, which everybody loved, to put "A" papers from any of the children on the kitchen wall. These and other changes began to make the individuals feel more like a family.

Within about five weeks, Onolee's depression began to lift. Her family reported that she seemed to be sleeping and eating better and to be less irritable. Her teacher reported that she had become more playful and that her concentration and work were beginning to improve. As she got better, the frequency of therapy was tapered down gradually, from one individual and one family session per week at the beginning to one of either each week, then to individual sessions every other week in which whoever brought Onolee would spend a few minutes alone with the psychologist, and then finally to once a month. After about a year, therapy was terminated shortly after Mr. B and Fran were married. The therapist told Mr. B and Onolee that life presented many challenges and if they felt "stuck" at any time in the future, and particularly if Onolee should experience a return of any of the depression symptoms they had identified, they should not hesitate to contact the clinic again. At the last visit, Onolee gave her therapist an ornament for his Christmas tree that her father had let her purchase. It was a big figure and a little figure holding hands.

Thinking about the Case

When is sadness just sadness, and when is it depression? The *DSM* requires a specific symptom constellation that includes at least four of the following nine problems: (1) pervasively depressed (or, in children, irritable) mood, (2) marked and pervasively diminished pleasure in usual activities, (3) changes in eating and weight, (4) changes in sleep, (5) changes in motor behavior, (6) pervasive fatigue, (7) feelings of worthlessness or guilt, (8) diminished ability to think or concentrate, and (9) recurrent thoughts of death or suicide. These symptoms must result in "clinically significant" suffering and/or impairment of functioning.

Major depression is different from bereavement, although people in mourning typically experience many of the same symptoms, including sleeping, eating, psychomotor, and cognitive problems. But a psychotherapist will diagnose major depression only if acute symptoms persist for longer than two months or if pervasive guilt, suicidality, or significant impairment in daily functioning occurs. Onolee actually managed the bereavement caused by the loss of her mother fairly well. She did not become depressed until additional life changes occurred. She easily met the criteria for major depression in that her symptoms were quite severe and resulted in functional impairment over several months. In addition, she had positive thoughts of death.

It is estimated that the prevalence of significant depressive symptoms (although not necessarily major depression) is from 2 percent to 5 percent in children of elementary school age. This percentage increases with age and leaps markedly in adolescence: Depression is relatively common. Fortunately, most depressions, in both children and adults, respond fairly well to one or another treatment, including medication, various kinds of talk therapy, family therapy, play or expressive (art or music) therapy, and group therapy. In general, the more obvious and remediable the stressor, the more likely that psychological or social therapies will be prescribed. When depression appears to arise out of the blue, medication may be more strongly indicated.

Interestingly, though, medication often helps as well even in cases like Onolee's where environmental stressors are clearly identifiable and biological predisposition to depression is absent. These data support the conclusion that brain biology can be affected by environmental stressors. If this is true, then it may be inappropriate to choose between a "nature" and a "nurture" cause for depression. It may be more reasonable to inquire as to the relative weights of each type of input or more practical to ask where intervention is most likely to be effective. While research indicates that several brain neurotransmitters, particularly serotonin, are depleted in individuals who suffer from depression, studies also suggest that both psychosocial and biological therapies are effective in the treatment of depression. This again supports a biopsychosocial model of the disorder.

Onolee's case is typical in that more than one type of treatment is often included in the plan. This is particularly true for children, where the involvement of the family is often critical to the success of treatment. Family therapy is a relative newcomer to the psychotherapy field, having begun in the 1950s and 1960s as a treatment for schizophrenia. There are many types of family therapy: Some focus on family communication patterns, some focus on realigning dyadic bonds in the family, some try to strengthen the parental unit, and some focus on behavioral reinforcement patterns within the family. Many, like the kind used with Onolee, blend a number of perspectives, depending on the particular situation involved. In any case, the therapist's knowledge of and respect for the cultural context that influences the family's values and behaviors are critical.

The Developmental Perspective

For many years it was thought that depression per se could not exist in children because they were too cognitively immature to have developed a stable (negative) self-image or to have an understanding of the future (necessary for the concept of "hopelessness"). Later, it was thought that depression in children could exist but only in "masked" form, showing up as irritability, aggression, or poor school performance rather than sadness.

It is now clear that abnormally low mood does occur in children, although the symptom picture is affected somewhat by developmental level. Preschool youngsters who have experienced a loss of some kind may seem sad and irritable, losing interest in play and social contacts. They may regress in behaviors like toilet training or thumb sucking and exhibit somatic symptoms like frequent stomachaches. Their symptoms are primarily behavioral rather than cognitive.

In older, school-age children behavioral regressions are less common, but cognitive distortions are added to the symptom picture. These youngsters may begin to develop a poor self-image characterized by guilt, overemphasis on personal weaknesses, and expectation of future failures. Onolee's frequent apologies are consistent with this phase of development.

By adolescence, when future orientation begins to develop, depressed youngsters begin to display hopelessness about the future, which can lead to more frankly suicidal wishes and thoughts. Where Onolee experienced a vague wish to join her mother in heaven, an adolescent might actually entertain the idea of killing herself. Naturally, the increased independence of adolescents and their more competent ability to plan complex behavior make the risk of actual self-destructive behavior much greater. Further, adolescents have a wider choice of behaviors that can distract them, temporarily, from their emotional discomfort. These include drug abuse, sexual promiscuity, and excitement-producing, high-risk behaviors. Once these behaviors get established, it is difficult to tell whether low mood precipitated them or the behaviors precipitated the low mood.

One further developmental effect should be noted: In early school-age youngsters, depression is distributed about equally among boys and girls. By adolescence the rate is substantially higher in girls and remains that way throughout life. Whether this is a result of biological or social factors, or a combination of both, is not yet clear.

Questions to Consider

1. Deciding whom to treat may be as important in dealing with children's mental health problems as deciding how to treat. Do you approve of the therapist's inclusion of Onolee's grandmother, of Fran, and of Fran's children in the treatment in this case? Why or why not? Would you have brought others in? Whom and why?

2. Some family therapists speak of the "identified patient" in the family. By this they mean the child (or adult) who displays symptoms that reflect dysfunction in the family system. Do you agree with their idea that the whole family is really the patient? Who do you think is the patient in the case of Onolee B?

3. Try to get an African-American perspective on this case from a friend or classmate. Are there cultural issues that may be relevant to Onolee's treatment? What might they be?

4. If antidepressant medication were prescribed for you, or for a person in your family, how would you feel about the recommendation? Why? How would you go about deciding whether to accept or reject it? Would you feel the same way if medication were being prescribed for diabetes? Why or why not?

5. Consider the "learned helplessness" model of depression, which posits that organisms that are exposed to uncontrollable noxious events show symptoms that, in humans, we think of as depression. How might this model be applied to Onolee?

13

BIPOLAR DISORDER:
THE CASE OF WAYNE N

WAYNE WAS COMPLETELY immobilized. Slumped in the armchair in front of the television, he felt as if he literally couldn't get up. He felt weighed down in part by the twenty-two pounds he had gained since August, but more so by the sense of doom that seemed to hover just over his shoulder, no matter where he went or what he did. Here it was February of his senior year of high school, and he had hardly touched his books since the end of Christmas vacation. He had no energy. He had no concentration. Nothing seemed fun anymore. He didn't feel like doing anything or seeing anybody. And lately, he had been wondering why he went on living at all. What, exactly, was the point? As the television flickered in front of him, Wayne found himself thinking about his father's shotguns and about how good it would feel not to cry himself to sleep at night or wake up before dawn, feeling panicked and enervated. The thought scared him so much that a few minutes later, when his mother, who had been worried about him for weeks, came in to check on him, he tearfully told her that he thought he needed help—that he was afraid he might hurt himself. Within eight hours, he was hospitalized so that he could be safe while treatment for depression was begun.

Wayne's parents were mystified by the recent change in him. He had been a B+ student, vice president of his junior class, and well liked by everyone. They described him as a highly responsible young man who mowed the lawn and tended the flowerbeds without being asked, worked a part-time job, and spent an hour a day playing with his nephew, his older sister's child. He was highly organized and efficient. He expected the best from himself and, sometimes annoyingly, from everyone else. He was also extremely family oriented, taking most of the responsibility for decorating the house for Christmas and remembering everyone's birthday with a card or small gift. He had always been full of projects and enthusiasm.

Wayne had seemed fine throughout the holidays, his parents reported, even though this was the first Christmas without his grandmother, who had died the preceding summer. This had been Wayne's first real loss, and he had taken it pretty hard. He had cried copiously at the funeral and for several days thereafter but then seemed to recover. Wayne had also broken up with his girlfriend of eight months in the fall, but that had not seemed to affect him much.

After the holidays he seemed let down. He had talked to his mother about how much he would miss his friends and family when he left for college. He confided in her that he felt like he didn't really fit in with his high school crowd and was afraid that he wouldn't fit in at college either. She couldn't imagine what he meant, since he seemed to be universally liked. She had tried to reassure him, but to no avail. Mr. N said that Wayne had seemed lately like an engine that was running out of gas. He moved less and less, slower and slower, until he could barely take care of simple things, like showering and homework.

Mr. and Mrs. N appeared to be in some conflict when they were interviewed by the hospital social worker. Mr. N didn't believe that Wayne would really hurt himself, and he hadn't agreed with the hospitalization. He could see that Wayne was depressed and needed help, but he found it hard to trust the care of his son to strangers. Mrs. N had tried for weeks to get Mr. N to see that Wayne was in trouble. She felt guilty that they had waited so long to seek help and angry at her husband for "always having his head in the sand." The tension between the two parents was palpable.

Mrs. N also felt guilty because she had experienced episodes of depression herself, generally in the winter months. In addition, her father and paternal aunt had had episodic depressions. Her aunt had been hospitalized at least twice that she knew of. She guessed that depression might run in her family and that she had "passed it on" to Wayne. If she had known that this would happen, she said, she would have thought twice about having children.

Wayne was both relieved and embarrassed to be in the hospital. At least here he wouldn't be expected to keep doing things that he just couldn't do. He didn't have to hide how he felt anymore—he could cry if he needed to. He could take a break from keeping up appearances. Still, he felt really tired and hopeless that he would ever feel better. Being hospitalized for mental problems confirmed his worst fears about himself—that he was, indeed, unable to manage the normal stresses of life like other people.

However, Wayne was surprised to find that within a few weeks he did feel somewhat better. His treatment included antidepressant medication, individual and group therapy in which he spoke about the loss of his grandmother and his feelings about going off to school, and tutoring so that he wouldn't fall too far behind in his work. He also read a book about depression and talked with his therapist about strategies for staying well. At the same time, his parents attended an educational group about depression in the family that was offered by the hospital social worker. There they discovered that people in other families had experienced many of the same feelings that they had. This helped them look forward for solutions rather than blame themselves and each other for what had happened.

When he was discharged, sixteen days after he had been admitted, he was no longer suicidal, although he still felt far from well. The discharge plan included continuing on medication under the supervision of the hospital psychiatrist and weekly psychotherapy with a psychologist in the community. His parents elected to continue to attend the support group so that their own concerns and questions could be addressed.

Life went along fairly smoothly for some months, until the day after graduation. Wayne had been up late several nights running, finishing his senior paper and partying with friends. His mood had been excellent. He seemed to have boundless energy, loads of enthusiasm, and a great deal of optimism. In fact, he had seemed uncharacteristically social, dating several girls at once, going out virtually every night, and conversing more easily than he had ever done before.

Following the graduation ceremony, Wayne and a group of friends went to the beach for an overnight bash. At the party, he seemed "revved up," despite the fact that he wasn't drinking or doing any drugs. He insisted on playing the guitar and singing (although he had no talent at either). He couldn't seem to be still or to shut up. This normally somewhat shy, always thoughtful young man was being totally obnoxious. When one of his friends suggested he "take it easy," Wayne hauled off and punched him. By the time they got him home, he was blithering. Alternately singing and cursing, making no sense, he had been almost impossible to restrain in the back seat of the car. By that evening, he was back in the hospital.

This time, Wayne was diagnosed as having bipolar disorder (previously termed manic depression). His antidepressant medication was lowered and then stopped, and a new medication, lithium carbonate, was added. He was also given something to sedate him a bit and help him think more clearly.

For a few days, Wayne was too agitated and restless to participate in much therapy. His concentration was poor and he was easily distracted, both by things that were going on around him and by his own thoughts. Once he had had to be isolated for a couple of hours after threatening to hit another patient who had been annoying him. But by week's end, he was again attending therapy and beginning to participate in discharge planning.

Needless to say, Wayne was disheartened and not a little confused. How could it be that feeling so good could be a part of an illness? Did he really have a chemical imbalance, as the doctors said, or a weak personality, as his father sometimes implied? Would he have further "attacks"? Would he be able to live any kind of a normal life? How could he explain his behavior (and his hospitalization) to his friends? Should he go off to college as planned, or should he stay at home with his family, where at least he would be safe? Would life, in fact, be worth living? For Wayne, as for most young people who suffer from affective disorders, recovery would mean far more than taking medication: It would mean courageously confronting questions like these and mastering the challenges that they posed.

Thinking about the Case

Bipolar disorder is diagnosed when episodes of major depression are interspersed with episodes of clear-cut mania (in Type 1 disorder) or elevated, but not quite manic, moods (in Type 2 disorder). Like schizophrenia, bipolar disorder affects approximately 1 percent of the population, has its peak onset in mid to late adolescence or young adulthood, and afflicts males and females equally often. Note that this contrasts with unipolar depressions, which are diagnosed in women far more often than in men and which have a wider age of risk.

Wayne's presentation is not atypical. It may be that his "normal" state was mildly hypomanic—that is, more active and energetic than normal but not problematic. Then, without warning or specific precipitant, he became seriously depressed. Following a period of apparent improvement, he experienced a manic episode that finally clarified the diagnosis. In people with underlying bipolar disorder, antidepressant medication can precipitate a manic episode. This is probably what happened to Wayne.

Bipolar disorder is far from benign. Manic episodes, characterized by euphoric mood, grandiosity, irritability, racing thoughts, frenetic activity, impulsivity, and markedly impaired judgment, can significantly interfere with an individual's ability to work and to sustain meaningful relationships. Depression, with its concomitant decrease in motivation, socialization, and activity, also takes a heavy toll on functional ability. Perhaps it is not surprising to find that rates of divorce, alcoholism, and suicide are all elevated in individuals with bipolar disorder.

Bipolar disorder tends to remit and recur, with episodes lasting from several days to several months, generally with periods of normal functioning in between episodes of illness. In some unfortunate individuals, the illness is of a rapid cycling form, in which episodes of depression alternate with episodes of mania in quick succession, often with little or no respite.

Luckily, in about 80 percent of sufferers, bipolar disorder can be contained by the medication, lithium carbonate. Lithium, originally used as a table salt substitute, not only helps bring manic episodes to an end, but when used continuously prevents the emergence of both manic and depressive episodes in most vulnerable individuals. However, the side effects of lithium can be quite serious. Any prescription for it requires careful medical supervision and regular blood work to ensure that the dosage is correct.

What about the 20 percent of people with bipolar disorder who are not helped by lithium? Some of these get some relief from anticonvulsant or antipsychotic drugs. But many, unfortunately, are faced with multiple hospitalizations and a fairly chaotic life.

The success of lithium points to a biological basis for bipolar disorder, and current science supports this assumption, although the exact cause has not yet been determined. Some researchers hypothesize that the defect lies in normally self-correcting biological processes that govern mood states, allowing moods to overshoot the mark during corrections from sadness to happiness. In any case, research indicates that individuals are genetically vulnerable to the disorder. Identical twins have five times the concordance for bipolar disorder than do fraternal twins, and relatives of individuals with bipolar disorder have five times the normal 1 percent risk for developing the disorder.

Not yet answered is the question of whether bipolar disorder and unipolar depression are biologically related. Are they distinct disorders or do they lie along a single continuum? Future research will, no doubt, clarify this issue.

The Developmental Perspective

While children as young as six are occasionally diagnosed with bipolar disorder, the large majority of the cases emerge when youngsters enter adolescence or young adulthood. This may be partially because manic symptoms in chilldren, including irritability and frenetic behavior, can be mistaken for developmental perturbations. For example, parents, and even pediatricians, might say, "He's going through a naughty stage," or "She's just upset over parental conflicts." Sometimes, the same symptoms are mistaken for attention-deficit hyperactivity disorder because the youngster seems to be constantly in motion. In addition, the grandiosity that is often the hallmark of bipolar disorder, such as thinking that one is an astronaut in training, will seem, in younger children, like age-appropriate play or fantasy. So perhaps the illness is more often overlooked in preadolescent children. On the other hand, it is possible that biological changes associated with adolescence somehow trigger the disorder. It is also possible that the social demands of adolescence—the need for increased autonomy, judgment, and perseverance, for example—generate stress that precipitates the disorder in a genetically vulnerable person.

How might the age at which bipolar symptoms emerge affect development? One might hypothesize that the earlier the illness surfaces, the greater will be its effect on the developing personality, as younger children have fewer emotional and cognitive skills to draw upon. However, the enhanced vulnerability of adolescents to issues of stigma and social acceptance, as well as to issues of autonomy and independence, makes any newly emerging disorder, physical or "mental," a significant problem during this stage of development. Adolescents will be particularly challenged to incorporate the illness and the need for long-term medication into their developing self-image, more so than younger children. Therefore, treatment personnel must make special efforts to involve adolescent patients in education about the illness and in treatment planning. The more they perceive that they have choices, the more likely they will be to cooperate with treatment.

Questions to Consider

1. What kinds of data would help you decide whether bipolar disorder and unipolar depression are separate and distinct or related? Can you construct a study to address this question?
2. Some cyclical mood disorders seem to be seasonal. Sufferers

get depressed in early winter and manic or at least relieved of depression in the spring. Would you conceive of this as evidence for a biological, environmental, or biopsychosocial model? Why?

3. Psychoanalytic explanations of bipolar disorder hypothesize that mania is a psychological defense against underlying depression. What sorts of data might help you decide whether this is a feasible explanation?

4. Even a distinctly biological disorder can have psychological consequences. Consider the psychological and social factors that might affect whether a person would make a good or poor adjustment to a diagnosis of bipolar disorder. How would you predict that Wayne will adjust to his illness? Do you think he will take medication as prescribed, modify his stressful lifestyle patterns, and participate in psychotherapy? How might he react to the stigma and limitations associated with his disorder? How might you react under the same circumstances?

5. There is evidence that many successful people, including Abraham Lincoln, Winston Churchill, and Theodore Roosevelt, may have had bipolar disorder. What are some reasons that this might be so? Might this have any implications for creativity in relatives of people with bipolar disorder?

14

A DYSTHYMIC ADOLESCENT:
THE CASE OF MONICA M

MONICA HUDDLED INTO the corner of the sofa in the waiting room. With her head virtually shaved, baggy clothes, combat boots, and no makeup, this sixteen-year-old tenth-grader looked like a lost waif. She had been referred for psychological evaluation and treatment by her school because she had many absences and because she appeared sad and anxious almost all of the time. This was not the first time that Monica had seen a mental health professional, nor was it to be her last.

Monica is an only child who resided with her mother at the time of the evaluation. Her father, who had left the family when Monica was seven, is remarried and has two additional children. When her parents separated, her mother, who had previously remained at home, went to work full time. Monica's father had apparently been treated for depression, and Monica's mother has a history of alcohol abuse, with treatment instituted after her second "driving while intoxicated" offense. At the time of the evaluation, Monica's mother reported that she had not had a drink in over a year.

Monica had not had any major medical difficulties. She had several episodes of pneumonia as a child and had many ear infections in the first six or seven years of life.

Her mother reported that Monica had always had difficulty with new situations. For example, she adjusted so poorly to preschool, in which she was enrolled at age three, that her mother removed her and waited a year before sending her back. She also had trouble when her mom went to work, worrying constantly about her mother's welfare until she returned home in the evening. She had otherwise been a fairly easy child to raise: thoughtful and reasonably obedient.

Monica described herself as kind of a loner. She did have a steady boyfriend with whom she had recently become sexually active after going together for six months and on whom she depended a great deal. She also had one or two other friends, but most kids at the small-town school she attended hated her, even though she tried never to be mean to anyone. They called her "hippie," "druggie," and "freak." She felt she *was* a freak, although she didn't use drugs or even alcohol. She felt that she had never fit in anywhere. Nobody, except maybe her boyfriend, cared about her. She perceived herself as fat and ugly and stupid—all objectively untrue. She liked art a lot, and music and snowboarding, but denied being good at any of them.

Monica felt she got along fine with her mom but felt estranged from her father. They saw each other approximately once every two weeks, generally at his home or at a restaurant. She described her father as getting angry a lot and not being very good at talking. She felt that he was disappointed in her, although she didn't know why. She also didn't like her stepmother much and tried to have as little interaction with her as possible. When she was at her dad's, she spent most of the time playing with her stepsisters and trying to keep out of the way of the adults.

Monica freely admitted to feeling depressed. She cried a lot and often didn't feel like leaving the house; she had thought about suicide a great deal and had made several "plans" but had never acted on any of them. She wasn't having difficulty with sleeping or eating at present, although she had had problems in the past. Her concentration and memory were both "off," as far as she was concerned. She couldn't read or listen to music without having her mind wander off to things that worried or upset her. She hated school and virtually everyone in it—teachers and peers. On many school days she had headaches or stomachaches. Other days she simply could not make herself attend. She wanted to be home-tutored, but the school officials would not agree to provide this and her mother could not afford to do so.

Both Monica and her mother agreed that the symptoms of depression had been apparent for approximately four years, and they had gradually increased in intensity. Neither Monica nor Mrs. M was able to identify any specific precipitants for the worsening of Monica's mood, though, looking back, it was during seventh grade that her father's first new baby was born. About a year later, after feeling increasingly depressed and apathetic, Monica was evaluated and treated at the local public mental health center. She was serially treated with four different antidepressant medications, each of which seemed to help for a while and then lost effectiveness. She also saw a therapist approximately once every other week, but at the end of six months her condition remained unchanged and she dropped out of treatment. Since then, she had struggled along on her own, attending school sporadically and feeling fairly sad, lonely, and hopeless most of the time. Increasing conflict with school officials about her attendance and increasing desperation about how bad she felt had convinced Monica to agree to another mental health evaluation.

The evaluation methodology included interviews with Monica and with her mother. Her father was invited to participate but declined. He did, however, write a letter giving his impression that Mrs. M "babied" Monica because, in his opinion, she was "afraid to let Monica grow up." The evaluating psychiatrist also reviewed school records, which included data from educational and psychological testing that had been performed by the school psychologist. The recommendations were as follows:

1. One more trial of antidepressant medication, this time one with a significant antianxiety component. If it failed to produce sustained improvement at a therapeutic dose, an additional medication was to be added to augment the effect.

2. Weekly psychotherapy focusing on helping Monica to (a) develop strategies for managing anxiety and anger, (b) take less responsibility for her mother's welfare, (c) monitor and dispute repetitive thinking patterns that led to depressed feelings, (d) come to some peaceful resolution about her relationship with her father, (e) elucidate some personal goals toward which she could work, and (f) develop a more realistic appraisal of her strengths and weaknesses.

3. Sessions with Monica's mother, and perhaps with Monica and Mrs. M together to help mother and daughter each develop more self-identity and self-direction.

4. Continuing attempts to involve Mr. M in consultation and treatment planning in the hopes that he would take more responsibility for his relationship with his daughter. If possible, conjoint sessions should be held to help father and daughter increase their level of comfort with and understanding of each other.

Sometimes even the best laid plans can go awry. Monica initially accepted the treatment plan, started the new course of medication, and began to meet weekly with the therapist. As she had in the past, she experienced some initial improvement in mood and was even able to attend school more regularly for a while. But then she began to complain that the medication was making her feel spacey and disoriented. Her mother reported that her crying jags were beginning to increase in frequency and in intensity again. Demoralized and frustrated, Monica stopped the medication on her own. For a while more she continued with the therapist, whom she liked and trusted, but this, too, failed to produce sustained improvement between sessions and was soon discontinued.

Monica returned once the following year to report that she had dropped out of school and was planning to get a diploma by passing a general equivalency examination at the end of the year. She was studying for this on her own with the help of her mother's new boyfriend. Then she intended to go to the local community college to study horticulture. Her boyfriend had gone off to college and she was even lonelier than before. She wanted to learn some "stress management techniques." However, she canceled the second appointment and has not been heard from since.

Thinking about the Case

Monica has a type of depression called "dysthymia." It is characterized by low mood that, while not as severely debilitating as major depression, can linger for a long time. Adults are diagnosed with dysthymia if they show symptoms of depression for two years; for children, the duration is one year. Monica also appears to have a coexisting anxiety disorder manifested by her repetitive separation problems and by habitual worrying that is severe enough to interfere with her concentration and sleep. It is not unusual for dysthymia to co-occur with other psychological disorders: It is often found in conjunction with anxiety, personality disorders, and substance abuse.

Both nature and nurture advocates would have a convincing case in looking for the cause or causes of Monica's symptoms. Parental depression and parental alcoholism both predispose to depression in children, and Monica has both. The route of transmission might be partially genetic. Her dysthymia might also be partly learned, in that parents who are depressed or alcoholic may model depressed behavior and may also be unable to meet a child's needs for attention and nurturance. Monica might have learned some of her mother's depressed cognitions (e.g., that one is unable to meaningfully affect one's life or that the future is hopeless). Certainly her parents' lack of nurturance would exacerbate a low mood.

Family systems theorists would look at the role the child's symptoms play in the family as a whole. They might speculate that because she was an only child, because her parents were separated, and possibly because her mother was drinking too much, Monica might have become an inappropriate focus of her mother's attention, thereby exacerbating Monica's problems with separating. These theorists would hypothesize that Monica's mother "needed" Monica to remain dependent and helpless so that Mrs. M would have something to focus on besides her own dysfunction. Monica's problems would also allow her mother to remain connected to her ex-husband—by having his leaving the family to blame for Monica's depression.

In fact, the marital dissolution and Mr. M's subsequent remarriage might have contributed to Monica's depression and might be implicated in the maintenance of the symptoms over time. The affection and esteem of fathers contribute to the development of positive self-image in girls. Monica appears to have had less of this than would have been optimal. In addition, children sometimes feel that parental separation is somehow their fault. Perhaps Monica felt responsible for her mother's suffering. Guilty feelings could be relevant to poor self-esteem and to anxieties about her mother's welfare.

Finally, social factors are implicated in Monica's misery. Having been teased as a younger child, possibly because she was the kind of sensitive youngster from whom others can always get a response, Monica developed an out-group style of dress and behavior that, in circular fashion, further reinforced her isolation by others and her feelings of alienation.

In general, the longer one has had any mental health problem and the more pervasive the problem, the more persistent it is likely to be. Therefore, dysthymia is fairly resistant to treatment. Sometimes antidepressant medications provide some relief. The newer selective serotonin reuptake inhibitors (SSRIs), in particular, may be helpful to some people with long-standing depressive syndromes. However, neither these nor other antidepressants appeared to be helpful to Monica (although we don't know whether she was taking any of them long enough to receive an adequate trial). Individual cognitive psychotherapy may be helpful in isolating and combatting unrealistically negative perceptions about oneself, others, and the future. As suggested by Monica's psychiatrist, family sessions may help parents to more effectively support a child's emotional growth and development.

The case of Monica M illustrates the point that when there are a number of different causes, all acting simultaneously, symptoms may be particularly resistant to change. Her father's distance and disapproval, her mother's neediness, Monica's temperament, the critical behavior of her peers and teachers, and the developmental stresses imposed by adolescence combine to maintain her negative cognitive style and her depression.

The Developmental Perspective

While there is no separate category for dysthymia in children, developmental factors in symptom development are acknowledged in *DSM-IV* by allowing the diagnosis to be used when the primary mood is irritable rather than frankly depressed. By adolescence, however, depressed mood is apparent in dysthymia, as are the characteristically depression-generating thoughts about oneself, one's world, and one's future.

Self-image develops gradually throughout the school years, and by the end of adolescence it is relatively stable. In healthy youngsters there is a certain amount of anxiety associated with the increased demands for social skills and the increased importance of social success that mark the passage through adolescence. Self-evaluation can swing fairly widely depending on events of the day. A social success causes euphoria, whereas a social gaffe produces despair. Youngsters who are vulnerable to social failure, because of shyness, obesity, awkwardness, or a host of intellectual, physical, or social differences, might do fine in younger years but might begin to suffer at the hands of peers during adolescence.

By mid-adolescence, Monica's self-image was rigidly distorted in a negative direction and fairly impervious to new information (such as the fact that her boyfriend thought she was interesting and worthwhile). She perceived herself as having negative traits that she did not in fact have. She thought of her future as bleak. She assumed that virtually no one did (or could) care about her. Note that these perceptions lead to a self-fulfilling prophecy: The distorted cognitions lead to socially withdrawn behavior, which leads to further isolation, which leads to further negative self-perceptions. Once this pattern is set into motion, it is difficult to disrupt.

Note also that Monica thought more specifically about suicide as an actual action than did Onolee (Case 12), even though both were quite depressed. The enhanced ability to conceptualize, plan, and carry out behavior in adolescence increases the risk for self-injurious behavior. The younger child may wish to die, but the adolescent is able to act more successfully on the wish. Monica's refusal to go to school and her odd dress are other examples of depression-related behaviors that are unavailable to younger children.

Of course, adolescents also have the ability to engage in positive, depression-countering behaviors. A boyfriend, for example, can repair some of the damage to self-esteem that was caused by an emotionally absent father. Excellence in a sport can compensate for mediocre academic performance. Therefore, the adolescent's enhanced ability to act on his or her environment is both an opportunity and a risk.

Questions to Consider

1. Do you think it possible that Monica's anxiety disorder is primary and that her depressive symptoms arose later as a secondary problem? How might having an anxiety disorder predispose a person to depression? (Hint: Consider self-image as one of the intervening variables.)

2. What do you think are Monica's chances of continuing to struggle with depression into adulthood? Which factors that may be maintaining her current depression are likely to change as she ages? Which of them will remain?

3. Do you know anybody with a generally negative outlook? How does this person affect your own mood and your interest in spending time together? How might your (and other people's) reactions to him (or her) reinforce the way he sees himself and the world?

4. Maternal depression and parental criticism have both been shown to predispose youngsters to depression. What would learning theory have to say about this? What would psychodynamic theory contribute?

15

ADJUSTMENT DISORDER
WITH DEPRESSED MOOD:
THE CASE OF JOEY C

JOEY C WAS seven years old and just starting second grade when his parents split up. He'd had no warning. There had been no fighting or hollering. One day his father was just gone. His mom told him that his dad went to live with another lady, a lady who had two children of her own. He would likely pick Joey up for visits, she said, but she wasn't sure when yet. She seemed more tired than upset when she told him, but her nose and eyes were red and Joey wondered if maybe she'd been crying. He'd never seen his mom cry, and it scared him. When he started to cry himself, his mom gave him a hug and then told him to go get started on his homework.

Joey had trouble sleeping that night and for many nights thereafter. He began wetting the bed intermittently, something he had not done in over two years. He had a repetitive "sad dream" from which he often awoke in tears. In it, his father and he are building a sand castle together at the beach. All of a sudden his father seems to be deaf—he stops responding to anything Joey says. Joey shouts at his father, but there is no reaction. Joey reaches out and touches his father's shoulder, only to discover that what he thought was his father was just a sand statue. His father is not really there at all. Joey feels inexpressibly lonely in the dream, starts to cry, and wakes up.

By day, Joey seemed listless and tired. This once giggly and active child was now hard to engage. Instead of playing outside with the friends he had on the block, he seemed to prefer watching television alone. With his mother, he was cranky and demanding. Nothing seemed to please him.

Joey came into therapy three months after the separation, when his teacher expressed her concern to Joey's mom. His school work had deteriorated, but more than that, she said, he just seemed sad. He no longer volunteered for projects, he wandered around on the playground by himself during recess, and he was irritable and distracted. He just wasn't himself. Mrs. C acknowledged the changes in Joey. Indeed, she had seen them herself but had felt so guilty and helpless that she had tried to talk herself into believing that they were normal and just temporary. With a bit of encouragement from the teacher, she agreed to seek help.

The therapist learned from his interview with Mrs. C that Joey's dad had left the family emotionally as well as physically. He seemed more heavily invested in parenting his new woman's children than in maintaining strong ties with Joey. While he did pick his son up each week for an overnight visit, Joey had to sleep in his new "brother's" room and try to fit into the new family's routine. He never had private time with his dad, nor did he know how to ask for it.

The therapist also learned, more from observation than anything else, that Mrs. C still seemed "shell-shocked" herself. She, too, appeared listless and distracted. She was attending successfully to Joey's physical needs but had little to give him emotionally. While she understood that he was upset, she didn't know how she could help him and, in truth, she had barely enough energy to get through her own days. Her husband's leaving had left her financially strapped, so she had taken a second job. She had virtually no time to herself anymore. When she wasn't with Joey, she was at work.

Therapy had two goals. The first was to give Joey an opportunity to express more directly the sadness (and probable underlying anger, guilt, and fear) that he felt. In order to do this, the therapist taught Joey a game called "Tell Me a Story." In this game, the therapist would tell a story and Joey would have to guess how the protagonist (always an animal or child his age) felt. Then Joey would tell a story and the therapist would guess how the protagonist felt. In this way, Joey was helped to understand that it is normal and appropriate to have feelings in response to situations. He was also better able to label his feelings and those of others around him. Not surprisingly, after Joey and the therapist had played the game for a few weeks, the stories frequently revolved around separation and divorce issues. A second part of the game was added in which the guesser also had to guess what the protagonist did in response to the feelings he was having. In this way, the therapist began to model appropriate ways of managing sad or angry feelings. The therapist broke up the sessions a bit by also reading with Joey a book about marital separation from the child's point of view and by having Joey draw pictures about various situations in his life.

The second goal of therapy was to get Joey's parents to understand and respond more effectively to his needs. Recognizing that Mrs. C would be unable to do this until she felt a bit better herself, he recommended that she attend a support group for recently separated people, which she agreed to do. She also agreed to spend one evening a week socializing with co-workers or family, even if she had to get a babysitter for Joey, and to go bicycling with Joey for a half hour every day that the weather and her schedule would permit. At the therapist's suggestion Mrs. C's family physician prescribed an antidepressant medication for her, which seemed to lighten her feelings of listlessness and bleakness. She found, after taking the medication for about six weeks, that she had more energy, more enthusiasm, and the beginnings of optimism that she and Joey would not only survive but thrive.

The therapist spent more than half of each scheduled session with Mrs. C, helping her express her own outrage, sense of failure, and fears about the future. Gently, he suggested that she needed to be able to encapsulate these feelings so that they would not interfere with Joey's relationship with his dad. She and Joey's father would need to be co-parents forever, so they ought to make a good beginning, he suggested. Mrs. C could not help but agree, at least in principle.

The therapist also made arrangements to meet separately with Joey's father, who attended the session with his new mate. Mr. C expressed a great deal of ambivalence about how he should treat Joey. He wanted his future wife to feel confident that he cared about her and her children. He did not want her to think he was "unfairly" attached to Joey. On the other hand, he loved Joey and understood that he had a responsibility to remain father to him to the greatest extent possible.

Mr. C's new mate handled the issue well. With the therapist's guidance, she told Mr. C that she couldn't love a man who wasn't committed to his children, and she wanted him to be a good father to Joey. Together, they decided to turn a small study into Joey's room, so that he would feel more comfortable on visits. They also agreed that Mr. C would pick Joey up for dinner one night during the week, so that they could have some private time. Mr. C further offered to bring Joey to some of his therapy sessions, provided that Joey's mother agreed.

Therapy terminated after four months of weekly, and then biweekly sessions. By the end of therapy Mrs. C and Joey's teacher reported that he was substantially back to his old, zestful self. He felt more confident that his dad was still his dad, and he had learned that his mom's anger at his dad was hers and he didn't have to share it. He still got uncomfortable when she slipped and badmouthed his dad, but he was able to tell her and, generally, she apologized and tried not to do it again. He still wished that his parents had not separated, but he was now able to accept the current situation and go on with his own life tasks, essentially unimpaired.

Thinking about the Case

Adjustment disorder is diagnosed when a stressor can be identified and when the individual's response seems excessive to the stimulus or when functioning (social, academic, or vocational) is substantially impaired. It can be diagnosed in both children and adults. An adjustment disorder can be characterized by depressed mood, anxiety, and/or disturbances of conduct. When the primary symptom is depressed mood, as it was in Joey's case, the disorder may be somewhat difficult to distinguish from normal bereavement, on the one hand, and major depression, on the other. For major depression to be diagnosed, more prolonged or profound deficits in functioning would need to be identified. These might include weight loss, suicidal ideas, school avoidance, or psychomotor retardation, to name a few.

Why do some people develop adjustment disorders and others do not? In Joey's case, we can speculate that his parents' ways of coping with the separation made adjustment more difficult for him. Temperament (for example, flexibility in the face of change), previous experiences (for example, a history of previous losses), and adequacy of the social support network are also relevant variables.

The Developmental Perspective

Divorce is a pervasive phenomenon in our culture. Youngsters will react quite differently to parental separation depending on their developmental level. Studies show that children of early school age, like Joey, suffer more when their parents divorce than do adolescents, who are more likely to become angry but are better able to continue to execute their own life tasks without interruption.

Older children have more language, greater cognitive capacities, and more experience solving problems than do younger children. Adolescents are more able to understand that they are not at fault in the divorce, are more able to hold a stable image of an absent parent in mind, and are less dependent on their parents for their sense of safety in the world. The process of gender role modeling is also substantially completed by adolescence, so that self-image is less affected by loss of access to the same-sex parent through separation or through death.

Depression in young children like Joey is often overlooked, because these youngsters lack the verbal and cognitive skills to show the full range of symptoms. Still, their behavior changes in characteristic ways. They become irritable, negativistic, lethargic, and withdrawn. It is easy to see them as "bad" rather than "sad."

Depression in younger children is different in yet another way: It is more responsive to the environment than that of older children and adolescents. Since a negative self-image has not yet developed, younger children do not depress themselves with their own thoughts the way older youngsters do; rather, something bad needs to happen to them. In addition, they cannot compensate for the bad thing the way adolescents can. Therefore, treatment concentrates more heavily on modifying the environmental stressor than on modifying the youngster's thoughts and feelings. For Joey to feel better, his parents had to do better.

Questions to Consider

1. Some children who suffer a loss like Joey's display conduct problems: They may lie, steal, fight, or engage in vandalism. What might predispose a child to this kind of reaction?

2. What theoretical models appear to underlie the therapist's choice of interventions in this case? What aspects of Joey's developmental level influenced the therapist's choices?

3. Try to find a friend whose parents divorced when he or she was a child (perhaps you won't have to look too far). Ask what effect the separation had on your friend's feelings, self-image, and behavior both at the time and as he or she grew up. What were the most challenging aspects to manage? Why? How do you think your friend's stage of development at the time of the separation affected his or her reactions? What other variables seem relevant?

PART FOUR

Attention Deficit and Disruptive Behavior Disorders

———◄o►———

Talking back, defying parents and teachers, refusing to do chores or homework, fighting, sneaking, lying, even stealing. These are common behaviors of childhood. Sometimes a youngster exhibits more of these behaviors than is normal, getting into trouble repeatedly at home and at school. When this is so, a disruptive behavior disorder may be diagnosed.

Two of the disruptive behavior disorders described in the *DSM* are oppositional-defiant disorder, which is characterized by a pattern of negativistic, hostile, and defiant behavior that lasts at least six months, and conduct disorder, a more serious problem in which violation of the rights of others or societal norms repeatedly occurs as well. We have included an example of each in this section.

The two attention-deficit hyperactivity disorder (ADHD) cases presented include a youngster with accompanying conduct disorder and a case of ADHD that is not as severe in its behavioral implications. We present both to show you the full range of problems associated with this diagnosis. In both children, you will see the core features of ADHD: inattention/distractibility and hyperactivity/impulsivity. Diagnosing children as ADHD has been quite controversial. Some educators and physicians claim that it has been widely overdiagnosed and over-treated with medications. These critics suggest that psychosocial factors need to be given far more prominence than neurobiological ones in explanations of why youngsters fail to meet society's expectations. Some have even gone so far as to suggest that ADHD doesn't even exist. They argue that distractibility and disruptive behavior fall along a continuum rather than in discrete categories of "normalcy" and "illness." We hope you will struggle with these questions yourself as you review these cases and as you observe youngsters you grew up with as well as those around you.

16

OPPOSITIONAL-DEFIANT DISORDER:
THE CASE OF TIMMY G

TIMMY WAS A SMALL, slightly built nine-year-old boy who had been referred for mental health treatment by his parents, at the suggestion of his pediatrician. An intellectually gifted youngster, in second grade Timmy had been identified as having a reading disability. Despite receiving specialized educational services, Timmy was doing poorly in his third-grade class. The problem, as reported by his teacher, was that he rarely turned in his homework, and when he did it was likely to be sloppy or incomplete. He had also been referred to the principal several times in recent months for refusing to work on an in-class project and for repeatedly interrupting class discussions. He was fine, his teacher reported, as long as not much was asked of him and as long as things went his way. When they didn't, he quickly became sullen and rude.

The therapist chose to interview Timmy's parents before meeting with Timmy. Mrs. G, a teacher's aide in the same school district, confirmed that Timmy tolerated frustration poorly at home as well as at school. He seemed irritable and argumentative much of the time, fighting her over homework, household chores, and bedtime. When asked to describe his positive traits, Mrs. G hesitated briefly. Then she talked about his creativity and ability to work with his hands. He could also be pleasant at times and had a good sense of humor when he wasn't annoyed at someone or something.

Mr. G worked night shift as a prison guard in a nearby minimum-security state prison. He reported that he didn't see as much of Timmy's problematic behavior as his wife did because he often slept until after Timmy and his younger brother had eaten dinner. They only had an hour or two together as a family before the children's bedtime on weeknights. On weekends, Mr. G moonlighted as an emergency medical technician, so his contact with his children was, by necessity, fairly limited.

Generally, when Mr. G asked Timmy to do something, it was done, although often with a scowl, foot stomping, or rolling eyes. Mr. G considered it normal for a boy to resist doing what he was asked. He had been like that himself, he reported, and he was not inclined to worry about it much. His wife, he said, just wasn't firm enough with Timmy. She tended to use a disciplinary strategy she had learned about called "time out," a version of sitting in the corner, whereas he himself opted for a more activist approach. He felt that moving Timmy bodily from in front of the television when he resisted, or providing the occasional slap on the backside, was more likely to be successful.

The tension in the consulting room mounted noticeably as Mr. G offered these opinions in a manner that seemed to imply that any disagreement was patently idiotic. For a few moments, nobody spoke. Finally, the therapist commented that it was natural for parents to have somewhat different perspectives on a child's behavior. Mrs. G then muttered, "Yeah, his perspective and the wrong perspective."

What emerged in the ensuing conversation was that the marriage had been fairly rocky for some time. Mrs. G felt generally unsupported by Mr. G. She complained that he never took her out, never complimented her cooking or cleaning, and never bought her little gifts. Recently, he had even forgotten her birthday completely and seemed not to care when she felt wounded by it.

For his part, Mr. G felt that nothing he did was ever good enough for his wife. He worked long hours to support the family while she worked six hours a day and had summers off. He didn't hang out at bars. He didn't cheat on her. He tried to spend a few hours each week with her and the children. In return, she begrudged his hunting in the fall, nagged him about helping with housework, and fought with him any time he wanted to spend money on anything other than clothes and food.

At the end of the initial interview, the therapist suggested that perhaps they might begin with some sessions with Mr. and Mrs. G alone. The goal would be to strengthen the parental unit so that Timmy would face a more united front and so that home life would be less tense. While Mrs. G was willing to agree to this plan, Mr. G was not. He did not have the time, he said, to come for regular sessions. In his mind, Timmy's behavior was fine when he was around and it was his wife who needed the help. Further, he said, pointedly turning toward his wife, money was short and they could not easily afford extended therapy. Again, silence fell. Finally, the therapist suggested that they go home and think about how they might like to proceed and give him a call. Not surprisingly, he did not hear from them again.

Thinking about the Case

All children are oppositional from time to time. To receive a diagnosis of oppositional disorder, a child (or adolescent) must exhibit a pattern of hostile, defiant, and negativistic behavior that lasts at least six months. These children lose their temper easily and tend to be argumentative and even spiteful. They may behave in purposely annoying ways, refuse to do what is asked of them, and blame others when things go wrong. Unlike youngsters with conduct disorder, they do not consistently violate the rights of others; rather, they seem hypersensitive to making sure that their own rights (as they perceive them) are not violated. Oppositional-defiant disorder may co-occur with other disorders of childhood or adolescence. It is not uncommon for these children to be depressed, to have learning disabilities like Timmy's, or to have attention-deficit hyperactivity disorder.

An oppositional behavior pattern can result from an interaction of many factors: the child's genetically determined temperament, the adequacy of parental limit setting, the level of stress in a child's environment and the child's own strategies for managing stress, parental modeling and reinforcement of oppositional behavior, and peer group influences, among others. We can surmise, in Timmy's case, that his father's tacit acceptance of his behavior, his parents' inability to agree on how to manage his oppositional behavior, the stress imposed by his reading disability, and his own inadequately developed capacity to tolerate frustration are all implicated. The general level of marital discord and tension in the household and the absence of his father in his daily life may also play a role.

The two most common modes of treatment for oppositional-defiant disorder are behavioral treatment and family therapy. In behavioral treatment, parents and teachers are taught to reward cooperative behavior consistently and to ignore or punish oppositional behavior. Sometimes, a token system is used, in which a child can earn tokens with good behavior. The tokens can then be exchanged for a treat, a toy, or time spent alone with a parent in a special activity. For this treatment to work, the target behaviors must be clearly defined, the rewards must be things the child genuinely wants, and the system must be rigorously applied. For example, if a parent ignores most oppositional behavior but responds when the child escalates to the point of having a temper tantrum, the parent may be inadvertently reinforcing the tantrum with attention, thereby increasing the probability of its occurring again. A behavioral plan is virtually impossible to implement if parents undermine each other as Timmy's parents did. In cases like this, family-oriented counseling may be a preferable intervention.

Family therapy is based on the premise that the dysfunctional behaviors play a role in maintaining family homeostasis or that interactional factors are responsible for maintaining the behavior. One might hypothesize, for example, that Timmy's behavior serves a purpose in taking the focus off the marital problems his parents are experiencing. Or one might wonder whether Timmy is acting out (or imitating) Mr. G's anger at his wife. Or, more simply, one might surmise that reducing the level of parental dysharmony and increasing their ability to coparent would help them respond more effectively to Timmy's provocative behavior.

Both forms of treatment can be combined in what is called "behavioral family therapy." In this form of treatment family members come together to develop a behavioral plan in which the target behaviors, the rewards, and the punishments are all spelled out, often in the form of a written contract.

Timmy's case illustrates how the choice and timing of a treatment intervention can make a difference in a case. The therapist's decision to offer marital therapy so early in his relationship with Mr. and Mrs. G was probably, in hindsight, an error. In doing so, he appears to have scared them off. He might have done better to meet with Timmy first or to try a few sessions with the whole family present, keeping the focus on Timmy rather than on the marriage. In general, it is best to start with what the family defines as the problem, rather than what the therapist thinks is the "real" problem.

The prognosis for untreated oppositional-defiant disorder is extremely variable. In some cases, youngsters progress to more serious rule-breaking behavior as they get older. They may then be rediagnosed with conduct disorder. In other cases, they seem to grow out of it, becoming more tolerant of limit setting with time. Often, these youngsters will continue to have similar problems into adulthood: conflicts with bosses and loved ones, difficulty accepting responsibility, sullen resistance to perceived demands. Generally, the less severe and prolonged the behavior, the better the prognosis.

The outcome of treated cases is also variable, depending on which and how many of the variables are sustaining the behaviors. The higher the parents' level of motivation, intelligence, and ability to cooperate with each other and with the treatment plan, the better the prognosis. The fewer the outside stresses and the stronger the outside supports experienced by the family the better. Prognosis will also be improved to the extent the therapist makes an accurate assessment of the biological, psychological, and environmental factors involved and develops a plan that addresses as many of these as possible.

The Developmental Perspective

Everybody has heard of the "terrible twos." At about this age, children learn the meaning (and power) of the word "no." They begin to assert their own independence and resist attempts by others to control them. Thus, oppositionality is a universal and normal development. At this point, cultural and social determinants begin to exert an impact on the child's development. Some cultures (and some parents) rigorously enforce discipline, teaching children to subordinate their needs and wishes to those of the parents. Others value independence and initiative and will tolerate more defiance from children. In any case, the pre-school years are taken up by socializing children to act appropriately in a variety of settings.

Entering school presents another challenge for youngsters. Now they must conform their behavior to the demands of a new set of adults (and increasingly to peers as well). If their previous socialization has prepared them well and their own temperament allows them to tolerate frustration, they will make this transition smoothly, treating their teachers with the same respect and compliance they have learned to apply to their parents. If, on the other hand, they have been inade-quately socialized (or socialized to a set of rules that is markedly different from that found in school) or have impaired ability to delay gratification of their own needs, they may have a difficult time accom-modating themselves to the level of behavioral self-control required by the school setting.

Even if a child has managed the transition to school well, entering adolescence presents another adaptive challenge. Here the youngster's job is to become an independently functioning adult, relying more and more on his or her own judgment than on that of others. Therefore, it is common for parents to see another surge of oppositionality from about thirteen through about sixteen or so. Youngsters of this age often think of their parents as dumb, outdated, embarrassing, and overcontrolling. They resist doing what is asked of them, because it seems to them a threat to their ability to choose for themselves what they will do. They argue, pout, and sometimes defy in an attempt to develop confidence in themselves.

Again, cultural and familial values will have an enormous influence on how youngsters travel through this developmental phase. In some cultures (and in some families), overt oppositionality is the exception rather than the rule, whereas in others the opposite is true. The child's own temperament and psychology will also affect this journey. Generally, youngsters who have been relatively mature, successful, and self-confident proceed through adolescence with less defiance, probably because they have less need to prove themselves to themselves. Children who have had difficulties finding a successful niche for themselves during the earlier school years may, at adolescence, identify with a more marginal peer group, in which oppositionality to the dominant culture is the badge of identification. These youngsters are then at greater risk for difficulties as they move through the developmental tasks of the adolescent years. They may, for example, devalue education and drop out of or do poorly in school or they may become involved in self-destructive substance abuse. Again, parents who are able to maintain standards while showing increasing flexibility and willingness to allow their growing children to make and take responsibility for decisions will minimize stimuli for oppositionality.

Questions to Consider

1. What do you think Timmy's prognosis is? Why? If you think his prognosis is poor, what might be done to change it?

2. Everybody knows someone who is oppositional by nature. Whom do you know who is like this? What biological, social, or psychological factors have you assumed were implicated in his or her behavior?

3. How did your own parents handle oppositional behavior in you and your siblings? What were the strengths and weaknesses of their strategies?

4. Consider movies, books, videos, television, celebrities, the news, and so on. Do you think American popular culture encourages or inhibits oppositional-defiant behavior? Give examples to support your opinion. If you wanted to reduce oppositionality in adolescents, would you change the culture in some way? How?

17

ATTENTION-DEFICIT HYPERACTIVITY DISORDER: THE CASE OF JOSH D

JOSH WAS THE much-wanted, firstborn child of Jim and Peggy D. Jim was a freelance graphic artist and Peggy, before she took time off to have Josh and his sister, had been a practicing obstetrician-gynecologist. Peggy had had an uneventful pregnancy with Josh and had delivered him at term without medication.

Both parents described Josh as a bright and active toddler. He exhibited an unusually large vocabulary from an early age and a lively curiosity about the world in which he lived. He was always making something, exploring something, or asking questions. He saw and heard everything. Their only complaint was that he didn't seem to need much sleep. He was up with the birds each morning, riding into their bedroom on his tricycle, playing "It's a Small World" on his tiny tape player. And though you'd think that a child who awakened at 4:45 A.M. each morning would need to sleep during the day, Josh rarely did. On car trips, when most youngsters would be lulled to sleep by the motion and hum of the engine, Josh needed to be amused constantly and he never stopped talking. He seemed to suffer from the confinement of the car seat more than most children, and his parents soon learned to limit their out-of-town traveling.

Peggy was relieved when Josh began his half-day kindergarten. Now at least she could get a nap! Josh did all right there, but he frequently complained that he didn't like it. His teacher said that he always made interesting comments in discussions and was a leader during free-play games, but he got bored easily. For example, during story time he often commented aloud on the story at inappropriate times. At other times he seemed not to be paying attention at all—he couldn't answer even simple questions about the story. And whenever he didn't like the activity of the moment he'd wander off and often end up drawing attention to himself by trying to kiss one of the girls or by making funny faces.

The situation didn't improve in first grade. While a bit slow in picking up reading, Josh seemed to be learning well. However, his work was messy and sometimes not finished. His teacher, a fairly disciplined and stern woman, did not take kindly to his telling her that he knew the answers and didn't see why he had to practice the same things over and over again. She expected his homework to be done and to be done neatly. She told his parents that Josh was immature, unmotivated, disruptive, and undisciplined. Josh, in turn, hated her. In March, he tried to convince several other children in the class to go with him to the principal to complain about her, but he got no takers.

Josh's parents discovered that getting Josh to do homework could be a grueling and frustrating prospect. They took turns supervising him, because neither could stand the frustration two nights in a row. And they tried everything—cajoling, bribing, threatening—but nothing worked consistently or for very long. Sometimes he lost his temper, tearfully shouting, "I can't do it. I'm just too dumb!" Secretly, Jim and Peggy had some sympathy for him, because they, too, thought that his teacher was too heavily focused on rote learning and too little on creative expression. Still, they felt they had to support her in dealing with Josh so that he wouldn't receive mixed messages about what was expected. Their one success was in getting Josh to read for twenty minutes each evening. Guiltily, they bribed him: a dollar per evening. Josh earned a video game that way and his reading improved.

As the end of the school year approached, Peggy became genuinely worried as she observed their normally enthusiastic, effervescent child becoming moody and irritable. She shared with her husband her concern that Josh might be suffering from attention-deficit hyperactivity disorder, which she had learned about from pediatrician colleagues.

Jim indignantly denied that anything might be wrong with Josh, with the exception of having a witch for a teacher. He, too, had had problems in school and had even "flunked" kindergarten because he was judged to be too immature at age five to begin school. He had learned to read slowly and had thought of himself as dumb for a long time. He thought teachers were much too demanding of young children, expecting them to behave like "little robots."

Nonetheless, despite Jim's objections, Peggy approached the school psychologist and asked that Josh be evaluated. Because she was overloaded with mandated reevaluations of children with already identified special needs, the psychologist was only able to observe Josh in class briefly and speak with his teacher. She told Peggy that Josh was a talented, delightful youngster who might be just a bit immature. She assured Peggy that he would "grow into himself" before long.

Summer was a great relief for the entire family. Josh spent huge chunks of time outdoors with his friends, playing ball, swimming, and exploring, and he generally seemed much like his old self. His room was a mess, as usual, and he couldn't seem to find his baseball mitt or bathing suit when he needed them, and he sometimes annoyed his friends because he would daydream and miss a catch when playing right field, but he was mostly cheerful and giggly. The triumph of the summer was learning to ride his two-wheeler while all of his friends were still using training wheels.

Luckily for Josh, his second-grade teacher focused more on Josh's strengths than his weaknesses. She found him delightful and creative when a project interested him and he could remember his assignment and find the materials he needed in his overflowing bookbag. However, if he was not emotionally engaged with the task, he tended to lose focus, wander around, and disrupt other children's activities. She used a token system in her classroom so that each child could be rewarded for specific behavioral accomplishments. Josh earned stickers for staying on task and completing assignments. At the end of each week, Josh got to choose a small prize from his teacher's "surprise box" if he had earned ten stickers that week. In addition, Josh's parents received a daily report card letting them know how Josh had done that day and what his assignments were for the next day so that they could closely supervise his work at home. His parents instituted a reward system at home as well: When Josh had managed two "ten-sticker" weeks in a row, he got to suggest a special outing for the family such as a trip to the science museum or zoo.

Still, while all this careful programming did allow Josh to enjoy school much more, his teacher agreed with Peggy that his attention span and ability to organize himself lagged behind other children. Another meeting was arranged with the school psychologist, who now did a full evaluation. This resulted in a consultation with a neurologist, who agreed with the diagnosis of attention-deficit hyperactivity disorder of the primarily "inattentive" subtype. He prescribed stimulant medication and suggested that they return in three months. However, after one week Josh seemed tired and uncharacteristically tearful. When he seemed worse in the second week, his father was ready to give up on the neurologist and on the medication. Peggy prevailed on him to go one step further, though, and they consulted a child psychiatrist, who confirmed the diagnosis and suggested a trial of a different medication. He offered to see Josh weekly until a decision could be made as to whether the medication was helpful and to call Josh's teacher regularly to get her input.

This medication seemed to work much better. After three months, his teacher reported that his ability to complete assignments and to organize his desk and bookbag was much improved. She also noted that he was less "spacey" and more able to stay on task, even when he was mildly bored. His parents, meanwhile, were experiencing much less resistance from Josh about doing homework. At the same time, he seemed finally to be making some friends at school.

At follow-up six years later Josh was doing well at home and at school. A frustrating trial off medication in fourth grade had convinced even his father that his functioning was much better with the medicine than without, and no further attempts to withdraw him were made. However, at that time, his parents decided that Josh should receive some focused counseling designed to teach him strategies for organizing and remembering better, and that counseling was still going on at follow-up. Josh hoped that he would be able to do without the medication by the time he finished high school. On that score, the jury is still out.

Thinking about the Case

There are two core symptoms of attention-deficit hyperactivity disorder (ADHD): inattention/distractibility and hyperactivity/impulsivity. These youngsters are always on the go. Sometimes their parents describe them as "driven by a motor." They talk excessively, blurt out answers, have trouble awaiting their turn. They fidget and move around more than do other children. They have difficulty staying still. In addition, they have great difficulty sustaining attention. They lose things, do sloppy work, can't sustain mental effort for long, and are forgetful and poorly organized. It's easy to see how these children get labeled as troublemakers by their parents and teachers. Josh exhibited a subtype of the disorder in which he showed more of the symptoms of inattention and fewer of the symptoms of impulsivity. Children whose ADHD falls in the primarily hyperactive-impulsive subtype tend to get into more trouble: They may be aggressive with peers and engage in activities that are dangerous to themselves or others. Some children show approximately equal parts inattention and impulsivity: These are youngsters with ADHD of the "combined" subtype.

While the diagnosis requires that at least some symptoms be present before the age of seven, many children are not diagnosed with ADHD before they enter school. This is particularly true for the primarily inattentive subtype of the disorder because the more structured environment of school highlights the very skills that these children lack, whereas in the home environment these skills may not be as necessary. Thus, it is not uncommon for parents like Josh's dad to disagree with the diagnosis when the child functions acceptably at home but not at school even though the parent acknowledges that signs of distractibility and inattention are present at home as well. In contrast, children with ADHD of the primarily hyperactive-impulsive subtype or the combined subtype are often diagnosed as preschoolers and typically manifest obvious symptoms at both home and school.

The estimated prevalence of ADHD varies widely, but it is generally agreed that it is found in roughly 5 percent of children, with the rate in boys being three or four times the rate in girls. Among children referred to child mental health clinics, the rate is much higher, accounting for one-third to one-half of all referrals.

Not surprisingly, ADHD has a high rate of co-morbidity with other disorders. Approximately 30 percent to 50 percent of children with ADHD also have diagnosable oppositional-defiant disorder or conduct disorder (as in the case we present next). This is particularly common in children of the hyperactive-impulsive and mixed subtypes. Roughly one-fourth of children with ADHD have significant reading problems, language delay, or learning disabilities, and youngsters of the primarily inattentive-distractible subtype seem especially prone to developing such learning difficulties. Many more manifest lower achievement than would be expected given their I.Q. scores. As many as one-fourth to one-third of children with ADHD have problems with anxiety and/or depression as well.

In Josh's case, we could see the beginning of a depression developing in kindergarten and first grade as a reaction to negative social feedback and an increasingly negative internalized self-image. Luckily, his ADHD was successfully treated before this depression had a chance to become deeply entrenched. Other children are not so lucky. Their ADHD may not be diagnosed for many years. In other cases, the treatment may be less successful in modulating the youngster's behaviors and, in turn, the feedback he receives from others.

While opinions vary somewhat, there is reasonably strong consensus among researchers in the field that the cause of ADHD is primarily constitutional. There is strong evidence of a genetic basis for the disorder, with estimates of its heritability in the range of 50 percent. One might speculate, in the present case, that Josh's dad might also have had ADHD as a child. While the definitive biological cause of ADHD is still unknown, many researchers suspect that the disorder stems from some deficit in the operation of the parts of the brain (particularly the prefrontal lobes, caudate nucleus, and striatum) that control the "executive functions" of planning, organization, sequencing, and prioritizing of behavior. Clearly, environmental factors like poor limit setting and inconsistent discipline can also contribute to a child's failing to develop age-appropriate self-control, but we know that even parents with good child-rearing skills find it hard to set and maintain limits with a child who has ADHD.

Treatment for ADHD combines medication and environmental changes. Stimulant medications work in about 70 percent of individuals with ADHD to reduce hyperactivity and impulsivity and to increase concentration and task focus. When they are taking medications, children and adolescents with ADHD tend to be less volatile and aggressive, allowing them to behave more appropriately in social situations. They also show better completion of tasks and more attention for academic instruction. However, despite these well-documented positive changes, there is little evidence to support the notion that treatment with stimulant medications leads to a better long-term outcome. Studies to date have been unable to show that medically treated children have better long-term academic outcomes, peer relationships, and adult adjustment status than those who have not been medicated.

Among the psychosocial treatments widely used with youngsters with ADHD are behavioral modification routines in the classroom, similar to the one Josh's second-grade teacher instituted. In addition, social skills training and cognitive-behavioral treatment designed to get the child with ADHD to "stop and think" before acting are widely used, although there is little evidence that treatment gains generalize to everyday behavior. Finally, family-based behavioral therapy designed to teach parents how to give clear directives and to provide immediate and frequent consequences seems to be effective in reducing friction in the home and increasing compliance with requests. It may be that the success of these interventions results not because the child with ADHD is actually changing but rather because the environment is being structured to compensate for his disability. Children with ADHD do better when tasks are clearly mapped out, frequent reminders are given, successful task completion is immediately rewarded, and failures to complete tasks are met with negative consequences.

The outcome of ADHD varies widely. Not surprisingly, children like Josh who are not very hyperactive or impulsive and who have few if any co-morbid disorders do better than children with accompanying behavioral, learning, or emotional disorders. Of particular concern are accompanying conduct problems. Youngsters with ADHD and conduct problems (like Anne J, our next case) are at high risk for psychopathology in adolescence and adulthood. Substance abuse and serious, repetitive bouts with the law are not uncommon. Even among individuals without conduct problems, more than half of those with ADHD manifest some symptoms as adults. While they are not so obviously hyperactive, they often show problems with organization and planning and they tend to procrastinate, to make rash and impulsive decisions, and to experience trouble persisting in tedious, effortful tasks. They are likely to be absentminded, forgetful, and sloppy. How much of an impact this will have on their lives depends to a large extent on what kind of environmental demands are made on them. For example, Josh's father did well in his job as a freelance graphic artist and his home life was supported by a highly organized wife. Had he been in a more regimented job, or had he had to take care of his own household, he might have experienced significantly more difficulty.

The Developmental Perspective

Many children with ADHD first show symptoms of the disorder as preschoolers. Such youngsters are overly active, hard to discipline, reckless, disobedient, destructive, and distractible. They often have delays in language development as well. Their "terrible twos" are truly gruesome, and they wear their parents out. While it is normal for preschoolers to be active and distractible, the ability to sustain attention improves gradually over time. Children with ADHD improve in this ability as well, but far more slowly. As they enter and go through school, they continue to lag behind their peers in the "executive functions" of organizing, planning, and controlling their behavior. Because they continue to have attentional difficulties, they may begin to develop learning difficulties in the school setting. In addition, their problems with overactivity and impulsivity often result in their becoming the focus of recurrent disciplinary actions by teachers. Their tactlessness, emotional outbursts, ineffective overtures to peers, aggressive attacks, and poor sportsmanship often lead to rejection by peers.

Not surprisingly, a significant percentage of these youngsters develop a poor self-image and begin to associate primarily with other similarly impaired youngsters. Toward adolescence, as parental controls loosen, these youngsters may develop an antisocial self-definition.

As self-control continues to lag due to the ADHD, behaviors dangerous to self and others become a concern. These can include substance abuse (including during the operation of a motor vehicle), vandalism, and other criminal behavior.

Questions to Consider

1. Many children with ADHD have parents with ADHD. How would the symptoms of ADHD affect parenting skills? How might these deficits in parenting skills affect the development of children?

2. Some people have argued that ADHD is not a brain disorder but a culturally determined one. They suggest that the behaviors of children so diagnosed would have been appropriate in an earlier society based on hunting, protection of the clan, and other self-directed behaviors but are less optimal in an industrial society based on the repetitive performance of routine behaviors. What do you think of this argument? Why?

3. Do you have friends or family members who exhibit behaviors consistent with ADHD? How have those behaviors affected their social and academic success? How is it for you to interact with them?

4. Many individuals in jails and prisons have had undiagnosed or unsuccessfully treated ADHD since childhood. How does the existence of a neurologically based disorder that diminishes one's ability to plan, evaluate, and control one's behavior impact your ideas about criminal responsibility? How might society reduce the number of individuals with ADHD who are incarcerated?

18

ATTENTION DEFICIT WITH CONDUCT DISORDER: THE CASE OF ANNE J

A YOUNGSTER SAT, or rather sprawled, on my waiting room couch. A baseball cap, turned backward, hid whatever hair there was. Jeans many sizes too big, held up by a raggedy belt, T-shirt, and huge flannel shirt covered the rest. I found this an interesting choice of clothes, particularly since it was July and about 80°F outside. I couldn't tell whether the child was heavy or slight, old or young, male or female. I had been expecting a fourteen-year-old girl; since no one else besides this young person and a woman, who appeared to be a parent, was in the waiting room, I gave it a try. "Are you Anne?" I inquired, smiling at her. In response, she didn't move, not even a twitch. Instead, the woman jumped up and said, "Yes, she's Anne. I'm her mother, Mrs. J. Anne, for God's sake, say hello to the doctor."

Clearly, I had my work cut out for me. I gave Mrs. J an insurance form to fill out and asked Anne to accompany me into my office. I half expected her not to move, but after a tense moment she stirred and, at a snail's pace, stood up. Still not looking at me, she shuffled ahead and stood like a rock in the middle of my office. "Sit anywhere you like," I said. She collapsed into the chair nearest the door, head down, legs sprawled out. "I can see you're thrilled to be here. Must be you've been begging your mom to come, huh?" This caused her to look at me for the first time. "Yeah," she said, "you're fuckin' brilliant." This was the start of my therapeutic relationship with Anne, begun almost two years ago.

Mrs. J had called me at the suggestion of her family physician, who had actually made the referral almost six months before Mrs. J contacted me. Anne's mother said she was concerned that Anne might be smoking cigarettes. She was also worried because she had found a cryptic note in Anne's room that the school nurse had said might be related to Satanism. Finally, when Anne got caught shoplifting, her mother decided to get some help.

Mrs. J didn't really like the kids that Anne was hanging around with, although she didn't know them very well. She also told me that Anne had been diagnosed with attention-deficit hyperactivity disorder toward the end of the school year and had recently begun taking stimulant medication—at least on the days when her mother could convince her to do so. She was currently attending summer school for two subjects that she had failed during the regular school year.

I pieced together the following information from my first few sessions with Anne. Apparently, she had carved out quite a niche for herself in school as a troublemaker, goof-off, and class clown in response to feeling socially isolated, inept, and stigmatized. She had always been badly teased by other children and had responded aggressively: shoving, kicking, and punching. Her current nicknames included "Thunderthighs" and "Shim" (an especially hurtful contraction of "she" and "him"). She professed not to care what anybody called her, but at the same time, "People know better than to say it to my face— now that I kick butt." Actually, Anne professed not to care about anything, with the possible exception of her friends, to whom she had remarkable loyalty. In fact, she seemed to look for opportunities to defend her friends with her fists.

Anne "hated" her parents, who, she gleefully reported, would buy her whatever she wanted whenever she wanted it. She wanted no part of any other relatives, describing her grandparents as "jerks." She thought her teachers were "assholes." She delighted in frustrating and angering them, particularly those few who professed to like her or to see some talent or ability in her. These she went after with a vengeance, although her antics were sometimes too funny to take seriously. She liked art and did fairly well in it, but she thought that all of her other subjects were "stupid." Her teachers were split between those who thought she was a total loser and those who felt she was a disturbed but bright and engageable youngster who was masking very poor self-esteem with bravado.

I tended to share the latter view: I had to, really, because I planned to invest some time in working with Anne. Mrs. J agreed to bring her for weekly therapy sessions and Anne, when asked whether she'd agree to come, said, "I don't have a choice, do I?" And indeed she didn't.

Over the next few sessions, Anne and I got to know each other. She described hating to get dressed for gym because she felt fat and ugly. She had handled this by cutting gym class or "forgetting" her gym clothes. Forgetting was actually pretty easy for her: She forgot to do her homework, forgot to take home her assignments, forgot where her bookbag was, forgot to turn off the stove after cooking a pizza. She assumed that she forgot things because she was stupid. That's what her friends and even one of her teachers had said.

She also agreed that her outrageous behavior was a sort of test. If people could run the gauntlet of her hostility, she might, perhaps, "let them in." Still, she denied ever having hurt feelings. Instead she would "just let it roll off me" or, more often, "get mad." Anyway, she never sat still long enough to be bothered by anything. She was always engaged in activity: skateboarding, playing video games, or finding trouble with her friends. She seemed never to consider her behavior, either in advance or after the fact. She just did what she wanted at the moment she wanted to do it.

By the time school started, Anne's mom reported that she seemed less angry and "more like my Anne." Unfortunately, she said this in front of Anne, who responded by being angry, sarcastic, and almost mute through much of the next several sessions.

School did not go well, despite Anne's mother's optimism. In October, when five-week reports came out, Mrs. J discovered that, despite receiving resource room help, Anne was failing about half of her subjects including industrial arts and band. All of her failures were due to inadequate homework or what the teachers referred to as a "poor attitude." Shortly thereafter, her mother also discovered that Anne had been leaving school without permission. Anne had been intercepting the notes from school so that her mother would not catch on. When I spoke with Anne about this she told me that sometimes she left when something made her really angry. At other times she just wanted to have a cigarette. School bored her. She didn't really enjoy the in-school suspensions she was receiving regularly, but at least they enhanced her reputation with her friends. They said that Anne was fearless, she would do anything, and she didn't care what any adults thought or what punishment they meted out. She was invincible.

Meanwhile, my relationship with Anne was progressing. Even though she still professed to think that therapy was a waste of time, she didn't really protest coming. In sessions, she told me about worries about various friends who were anorexic or suicidal. She reported that each of her parents was having an affair and that they might separate. This latter message was delivered with a shrug of the shoulders and absolutely no discernible emotion.

My own impression of Anne's parents was mixed. At one point I discovered that Mr. J had been cashing and spending the money remitted to him for our sessions by the insurance company, the money that was supposed to have been turned over to me. Mrs. J got me the money—after a huge, loud argument in the parking lot outside my office. Mrs. J seemed more responsible, but she often backed Anne up in arguments with the school principal and had several times been quite belligerent with him.

No matter what I did, I was unable to get Anne to reveal any real feelings about herself or her own life. I must have heard "I don't care" five hundred times. When I discussed with Mrs. J my concern that therapy might not be useful to Anne, she reported that Anne had seemed less angry and defiant since treatment was begun and that her grades appeared to be improving. I had my doubts about that, but I was sure that Mrs. J was benefiting from having someone with whom to commiserate and share ideas about how to manage Anne's increasingly hostile behavior.

In May Anne casually reported, in passing, that her parents had indeed separated. She thought it was "cool." She also reported in the same nonchalant way that she had been sexually active with a neighbor boy at the age of nine. Recently, they had started "going out" again. She regaled me with stories of having sex at parties, often in view of others. I had no way of knowing whether these stories were true, but they led us to some discussions about sex, love, and relationships. Anne also described shoplifting escapades with her friends. She seemed to have no remorse or conscience about these. Indeed, she got a "rush" each time she left a store with stolen merchandise.

In June, Anne described being afraid to go on to ninth grade. She had figured out how to deal with the junior high principal, but she was sure that the high school principal hated her. I assumed that there was probably some truth in this, since her reputation would surely precede her into high school. She wondered whether she ought to refuse to take her finals. I suspected that the idea of being a small fish in a much larger pond was really the threatening part of high school for her. She, of course, denied feeling any such thing.

Despite studying hard at the very end of the year and getting passing grades in most of her subjects, she soon discovered that she had done too little too late. With her mother's permission, the school chose not to promote her to ninth grade because her grades for many of the courses had been failing throughout the year and her grades on final exams were not enough to bring them into the passing range. The principal was concerned that she would not be able to keep up in high school without an extra year of working with the resource room teacher. He also wanted to teach her a lesson: that she needed to do her work and obey the rules.

While well meaning, this decision turned out to be disastrous for Anne. Anne was furious, both at her mother and at herself. She was vociferous in her certainty that she was "a loser," who had no goals and no direction. She described herself as "a big, dumb moron."

Anne seemed depressed and angry through the next school year. She reported increased drinking and use of marijuana. In addition, she told me about several instances of vandalism, including a tire slashing and spray-painting the home of a girl who had angered her in school. At the holidays she talked about hating Christmas and hating her family. She felt her mother was preoccupied with a new boyfriend and her father was an "irresponsible asshole." She described feeling that she would not live through a full adulthood. Instead, she envisioned herself having a violent death, possibly related to alcohol or drugs.

Still, for the first time, she revealed that she was beginning to like and rely on me. She said I knew her so well that it scared her. I reassured her that I only knew what she was willing to let me know, but I was pleased that she trusted me enough to let me get to know her. At the same time, she let me know that she had become more willing to let people touch or hug her, something she had never allowed before. She told me that all the changes in her were my "fault."

Anne passed that school year and I began to have some faint hope that perhaps therapy might be making a difference for her. Over the summer she shared her increasing concern about her boyfriend's drug and alcohol use while continuing to regale me with stories, some clearly made up, of her own. At one point she told me that he had tried to engage her in a double suicide pact. She had responded in a surprisingly mature fashion, not only refusing but talking with his mother about her concerns about him. Later she reported that he had "cleaned up his act," but her own use of drugs was increasing.

As she had suspected, ninth grade did not begin well. Anne found herself in loads of trouble. Everything she did brought her a suspension. Her mother had taken a second job and was unable to provide even the minimal supervision that she had provided before. Her father had gotten a girlfriend and seemed in his own world. She felt abandoned, although of course she reported that this was "cool," because she could do anything she wanted. By November her functioning had deteriorated significantly and I was becoming increasingly worried about her substance use. Finally, in early December, after an incident in which Anne actually punched the school principal, Mrs. J and I decided, first, to vigorously pursue drug testing to determine the extent of her use; second, to get a psychiatric evaluation to see whether medication might help her control her temper; and, third, to place her under the supervision of the family court as a "person in need of supervision." This designation would bring her under the control of a probation officer who would have the power to insist that she receive drug treatment and who could remove her to a residential treatment program if she did not comply with reasonable demands at home and at school. Anne, of course, was furious with us, but despite threatening to run away or commit suicide, she showed up at her next therapy session. The outcome of this recent intervention is still unknown.

Thinking about the Case

Youngsters like Anne are common in mental health centers, special education programs, and residential treatment units. Like many such youngsters, Anne presented with what is often called "diagnostic co-morbidity." That is, she met the criteria both for attention-deficit hyperactivity disorder, combined type, and for conduct disorder. In addition to the negativistic, hostile, and defiant attitude of oppositional youngsters, a child or adolescent with conduct disorder exhibits gradually escalating levels of rule-breaking behavior. In addition, serious relational problems exist. These youngsters tend to lack empathy, finding it difficult to grasp a situation from another person's point of view. Worse yet, they seem not to care. Like Anne, they may be unable to develop genuine attachment to family members or even to family pets. They have difficulty sustaining friendships through differences of opinion or disappointments. Not surprisingly, they present a serious management challenge for their parents and teachers while often acting as a role model, however negative, for a subgroup of their peers. In addition, Anne could have been diagnosed as learning disabled, given her normal intelligence but woefully deficient academic skills, as having a substance abuse diagnosis, and even possibly as clinically depressed. However, by the time that Anne was finally designated as a "person in need of supervision," her conduct disorder symptoms were the most obvious and dramatic manifestations of her psychopathology.

The causes of conduct disorder are multiple and often overlapping. In Anne's case, both her mother and father had explosive temperaments and a somewhat disdainful attitude toward authority and rules. Her father's own history indicated the strong possibility of untreated attention-deficit hyperactivity disorder as well as a diagnosis of antisocial personality disorder. Thus, Anne's inability to modulate her anger could have been exacerbated through modeling as well as predisposed by inheritance. Research suggests that antisocial parents and parental violence are risk factors for antisocial disorder in offspring.

Anne's physical appearance and quick temper had made her the victim of constant teasing throughout elementary school. Her identification with a deviant peer group may have seemed to her to be her only alternative. In addition, her mother, at least, seemed ambivalent about Anne's behavior. Sometimes she laughed it off and complained that the school was being too rigid. At other times she got furious and screamed at Anne. In addition, because both parents worked and were preoccupied with their own emotional issues, Anne got little consistency of supervision or direction. When they separated, she got even less.

Sadly, the prognosis for conduct disorder is generally considered to be quite poor. While many strategies are possible, including individual psychotherapy (such as Anne received), family therapy designed to change the ways families interact, behavioral treatment in which rewards and punishments are used to modify behavior, and medications designed to treat underlying depression or to assist with anger management, none of these therapies has been shown to be particularly effective. Roughly one-third of children with conduct disorder become antisocial adults, and many others manifest a variety of other forms of psychopathology as adults. In Anne's case, an intervention of over two years yielded only marginal results. One could argue that the time may have been better spent on another youngster, but only hindsight is 20–20 when it comes to psychotherapy.

The Developmental Perspective

This case illustrates a far different developmental trajectory for attention-deficit hyperactivity disorder than the case of Josh D (Case 17). It illustrates the important interaction between biology and environment in how disorders express themselves in individual youngsters. Early ADHD of the combined type looks the same: The toddler is active, distractible, always on the move. In school, the extent to which these problems get in the way may depend, in part, on how attractive, bright, or engaging the child is, how tolerant and flexible the teacher is, or whether the child has special skills or talents that balance the deficits. Where Josh was bright and sunny, Anne was irritable, sullen, and unattractive. Josh's parents were both available and motivated to provide him with structure and educational enrichment, while Anne's were in conflict with each other and unavailable for supervision. Josh was diagnosed and treated in second grade, whereas Anne got labeled as a "discipline problem" whose attentional problems were not identified until junior high school. Thus, she had more time to develop a deviant self-image that blossomed into full-blown delinquency in early adolescence.

Whether or not attention-deficit hyperactivity disorder is present, conduct disorder, the precursor to antisocial personality disorder (previously called "psychopathy" or "sociopathy") in adults, tends to be apparent very early, at least by the early teens. These are the youngsters, like Anne, who show pervasive and serious disregard for the rights of others in addition to an inability to modulate or appropriately express anger. The earliest signs, often discernible from the preschool years, might include an unusual level of defiance, inability to tolerate frustration, destructiveness, and deliberate cruelty to animals or other children. As the youngster gets older and has access to more independence, rule-breaking behavior spreads to school and community. In elementary school these children may be verbally and physically aggressive toward others, lie, steal from their parents, and neglect their schoolwork. In adolescence, when youngsters become more mobile, frankly illegal behavior develops, including substance abuse, vandalism, stealing, and battering. Since this is the age at which peer relationships begin to supplant parental relationships in the lives of most youngsters, gangs may develop among children with conduct disorder. By this time, the legal system is generally involved, as the rule breaking escalates beyond parental control.

Interestingly, antisocial behavior in adults seems to taper off some after the fourth decade of life. While the basic antisocial orientation remains unchanged, the energy that fuels acting-out behaviors seems to diminish in middle age.

When one looks back at the childhood of an antisocial adult, one can often see what appears to be an inexorable progression of defiant, rule-breaking behavior, impervious to any attempted intervention. However, in some cases, individuals who have exhibited conduct disorder in childhood somehow manage to change course along the way; they do not develop antisocial personality disorder in adulthood and attain relatively good adjustment. In a famous thirty-year follow-up study of antisocial children, it was found that about 18 percent ended up without significant psychopathology as adults. In many of these cases, a decisive factor had been the forming of a long-standing relationship with a nondeviant partner. Perhaps in these cases the capacity for empathy, attachment, and conscience, which develops quite early in normal youngsters, had not been as compromised as in those youngsters with conduct disorder who continued down an antisocial pathway into adulthood.

Questions to Consider

1. Anne's treatment has not been very successful so far. Using hindsight, do you think different treatment decisions should have been made along the way? If so, what are they? What would you do now?

2. Would you consider Anne's prognosis to be good, poor, or intermediate? Why? Can you develop a biopsychosocial model of prognosis for youngsters who exhibit conduct disorder?

3. If you were the director of a community mental health center that had limited staff and a large case load, would you accept Anne for treatment? Why or why not?

4. Some people would argue that "conduct disorder" is not a mental illness at all and would be couched more accurately in social, moral, or legal terms than in medical ones. Do you agree or disagree? Why?

PART FIVE

Substance Abuse and
Eating Disorders

◄◦►

Experimenting with alcohol, marijuana, and other drugs is a pervasive feature of adolescence in Western culture. For some youngsters, predisposed by heredity, personality structure, or environmental factors, the normal progression from experimentation to either abstention or controlled, social, adult use of substances gets derailed and a substance abuse or dependence problem develops. Alcoholism is among the most prevalent and serious public health problems we face today. Addictions to and commerce in other drugs have contributed to the increase in violence and crime in our society, and all has strained the public health and penal systems. While many of the adolescents we describe in this volume exhibit both substance use ranging from experimentation to abuse and some other psychiatric disorder, we have decided to include one case here in which substance dependence is the primary problem. This case illustrates a number of the difficulties of treating a youngster who is involved with drugs: the difficulty distinguishing the drug problem from other possible problems, like depression; the difficulty gaining access to real data about what's going on; and the difficulty getting the youngster's cooperation with treatment.

We have also included in this section two eating disorders, bulimia and anorexia. For several reasons, they are linked by a common discussion of their etiologies, treatments, and developmental pathways following case #21. While the *DSM* does not combine eating and substance abuse disorders, we believe that you will find certain similarities between them. In both, denial is a primary mode of defense, blocking awareness of the need for treatment. A sense of feeling out of control, combined with sneaking, lying, and rationalizing, characterizes these two disorders. Both have their peak age of onset in mid to late adolescence and are highly responsive to cultural norms of behavior. In addition, some researchers have hypothesized that eating disorders are actually addictions.

19

SUBSTANCE ABUSE:
THE CASE OF CAITLIN A

CAITLIN, a sixteen-year-old high school junior, was first seen by the psychologist at the request of her mother, who was concerned that her daughter "can't find a reason to get up in the morning." It seemed that Caitlin was missing school frequently, and her normally stellar grades had dropped to mid-B's.

Caitlin appeared, in the first interview, to be very depressed. This strikingly lovely but washed-out teenager was tearful throughout most of the hour. She complained of sleeping poorly at night, feeling tired and tense all day, having lost her ability to concentrate, and finding no enjoyment in her usual activities. She admitted to having suicidal thoughts several times a week and to using alcohol, marijuana, cocaine, and hashish to excess. She said, "When I party, I drink until I can't see. I combine drugs. I drive when I'm drinking. I know it's dangerous. I think I don't care." Caitlin felt that she had been getting progressively worse for about three months and thought that the precipitants for her distress were the loss of her beloved brother and many of her friends when they all went off to college the previous fall. At the same time, her boyfriend, whom she considered her best friend, moved permanently to another state.

Caitlin's father owned the grocery store in the small town in which the family resided. He was a gregarious and well-liked man in the community, always ready to do a favor or join in some community service activity. Drinking beer and joking around were woven into the fabric of his days. Her mother was the personnel officer at the local hospital, bright, competent, and self-aware. The family often joked that Mrs. A was the brains and Mr. A was the beauty, at least in his own mind. The family history was positive for both mental illness and substance abuse. Mr. A had a cousin who had been depressed and committed suicide in his early thirties and a brother who was an alcoholic. Unbeknownst to her parents but well known to Caitlin, her older brother was a pretty heavy user of marijuana and alcohol. It had been he who had introduced her to the pleasures of "the weed" when she was thirteen years old.

Caitlin was diagnosed as depressed and arrangements were made for her to begin taking an antidepressant medication in addition to her psychotherapy. She was cautioned not to drink or use drugs while taking the medicine and she agreed to refrain from doing so. Therapy proceeded on a weekly basis, examining Caitlin's feelings about her relationships, the pressures she felt, how she saw herself, how she wished she could be. Initially, she appeared to make good progress, resuming school attendance, getting her work done, and feeling more optimistic, but then she seemed to run out of steam. An increase in medication seemed to be helpful and she again seemed brighter and more energetic.

During this time, she talked in therapy about feeling that her parents preferred her brother to her. She revealed a strong need to compete with others, as well as a brief history of bulimia that had apparently resolved on its own after a few months. Also during this time, she helped a friend through an abortion, showing an unusually mature sense of responsibility and judgment in helping her friend and her friend's parents communicate and support each other during the crisis.

Caitlin continued through the rest of the school year taking one step forward then another backward. At school's end she seemed generally more confident, although she still experienced some lingering lethargy. She felt that her relationship with her father had improved greatly, that she had worked out some self-definitional issues, and that she was generally more in control of her life. Then, after canceling a couple of appointments in a row, she dropped out of sight.

The Caitlin that returned, on her own, in October of the next year was a changed young woman. Looking haggard and weak, she admitted to "getting into cocaine pretty heavy" over the summer. She had lied to her parents repetitively about where she was and what she was doing, spent all of the money she had earned from her summer job and stolen from them to buy drugs, and put herself into several terrifying and dangerous situations in order to score drugs. She had stopped using them three days before her return to therapy but admitted to experiencing severe cravings for cocaine. She confessed that she had continued to use drugs throughout her previous course of therapy and that her apparent ups and downs corresponded to her periods of abstinence and bingeing. Despite her therapist's urging, she refused to enter a drug rehabilitation program, insisting that she could stop using on her own. She did agree to seek additional help if she relapsed.

Over the next several weeks, Caitlin remained abstinent but miserable. She expressed a great deal of self-loathing as well as projection of blame. She felt that she was wasting her potential and that her father accepted her only if she was meeting his standards for excellence. She avoided her drug-using friends but she missed them and her drug-oriented lifestyle. Not long after, she admitted to having used cocaine with a friend. Reminding her of her previous agreement, the therapist got Caitlin to promise that she would attend a meeting of Narcotics Anonymous (N.A.). Caitlin did go to the meeting, but her cocaine use escalated nonetheless. At the same time, her motivation for sobriety began to waver. She knew she had a serious problem but wasn't sure she wanted to quit. With her therapist she discussed and rejected various options including inpatient rehabilitation, intensive outpatient treatment, and daily N.A. meetings. It was too near the end of the school year, she said; she had too much else to concentrate on and "now's not a good time."

After two more fruitless sessions, the psychologist came to a difficult decision. She knew that Caitlin did not have the strength to ask for the treatment she needed. She also knew that Caitlin was deteriorating to a point of significant danger to herself. Thus, she informed Caitlin that she intended to mobilize her parents to help Caitlin get into inpatient rehabilitation. Surprisingly, Caitlin did not object. Wearily she asked, "What do you want me to do?" The psychologist said, "Go home and go to sleep. I'll call your mother."

Mrs. A responded to the psychologist's call with her usual calm efficiency. By the next morning, Caitlin was admitted to a fine adolescent inpatient drug rehabilitation unit in a nearby city. The treatment program consisted of drug and alcohol education and many hours a day of group therapy, in which youngsters confronted each other and themselves about their drug use patterns, the trouble drugs had created in their lives, and the difficulties they would have avoiding drugs when they got back "outside." They learned to identify internal (feeling states) and external ("people, places, and things") risk factors for drug use. In addition, some hours each day were devoted to schoolwork so that they could keep up with their classes.

Mrs. A stayed in touch with Caitlin's therapist by telephone for the next six months, talking about Caitlin's progress and asking for guidance about various issues, including the advisability of letting Caitlin move back home if she dropped out of the treatment program prematurely. Both parents were involved in the family component of

Caitlin's treatment, and Mr. A was being asked to come to grips with his own drinking, which was causing a good bit of friction within the marriage.

Caitlin's progress, like that of most of her peers in the program, was uneven. It included several runaway episodes, relapses, and one moderately serious suicide attempt. Nonetheless, progress it was, and Caitlin returned for a follow-up visit with her therapist close to her one-year anniversary of being "straight and sober." By this time she had finished high school and was planning to attend college and live with her aunt in a state many hundreds of miles from home. She had not needed any antidepressant medication since becoming drug-free. For her, despite the family history, depression seemed secondary to drug abuse rather than a separate, coexisting problem. She seemed healthy and happy and confident, so confident that she had recently begun to feel like avoiding her old rehab buddies. She found herself going to fewer N.A. meetings where she would run into them, and she wondered aloud whether this was a healthy impulse or just another form of dangerous denial of the unwelcome truth that she needed to monitor her cravings for drugs for the rest of her life. Only time would tell what the correct answer to that question would be.

Thinking about the Case

Substance use, abuse, and dependence are ubiquitous problems among school-aged children and adolescents in our society. It is not uncommon to find youngsters experimenting with cigarettes at age ten, alcohol and marijuana at thirteen, and cocaine, psychedelics, and other drugs soon after. Substance abuse can be primary, in that no other psychological disorder predates or causes it. Or it can be secondary, meaning that it is caused by or accompanies another disorder, like antisocial personality disorder or depression, among others. Finally, it can independently co-occur with another psychological disorder. In Caitlin's case, the substance abuse was primary and the depression was secondary. Her therapist had gotten it backward, treating the depression and assuming that the drug abuse would abate when the depression receded.

The meaning of drug use and abuse in adolescents is particularly problematic since some experimentation with drugs and alcohol is normative in this population in our culture. For one thing, distinguishing problematic drug use from simple experimentation is difficult. Some practitioners assert that any use in adolescents is problematic.

First, they are by definition engaging in illegal behavior. Second, drug and alcohol use can be dangerous in certain contexts (e.g., driving a motor vehicle). Third, substance use impedes the development of age-appropriate skills such as academic achievement and social problem solving. Finally, adolescents, while highly susceptible to the pleasure component of drug use, have not yet developed the planning and problem-solving skills necessary to foresee the possible consequences of their behavior.

Other clinicians prefer to evaluate the individual youngster's use pattern before deciding whether to focus on it as a specific problem. Also, figuring out which social and academic problems are related to drug use and which are related to underlying personality disorder or some other mental health problem is sometimes close to impossible.

Experts also disagree about when it is appropriate to refer a youngster for specialized drug treatment and when the use or abuse can be addressed in a more general psychotherapy context. Substance abuse experts assert that psychotherapy can inadvertently reinforce drug use by implying that the use is understandable and acceptable until the "underlying problems" are resolved. To some extent, this happened in Caitlin's case. Add to these problems the fact that most people who abuse substances deny the extent and breadth of the problem or are only too happy to deflect attention to another problem. Caitlin was more than willing to accept the focus on her depression, because the prospect of giving up drugs terrified her. It is generally accepted that substance abuse, when it can be distinguished from use, must be treated as a primary problem whether or not there are other primary mental health problems, because it creates additional problems of its own. Once a youngster begins a problematic use pattern, his or her peer group changes, interest in age-appropriate activities drops off, and prospects for a successful life begin to diminish. In addition, when drugs are taken to self-medicate, the use can mask or modify the symptoms of other mental health problems, making diagnosis of additional mental health problems difficult. Thus, drug use is common in individuals with attention-deficit disorder, depression, and anxiety disorders. However, unless these disorders were diagnosed before the onset of drug use, they cannot be diagnosed with any confidence so long as the drug use continues. So substance abuse, when it exists, must always be addressed in any mental health treatment plan. There are even specialized programs for individuals with "dual diagnosis" of psychosis, depression, or anxiety disorders and substance abuse.

Many possible causes of substance abuse and dependence have been studied. Research has demonstrated a genetic predisposition for alcoholism, as well as a familial relationship between alcoholism and depression. Parental, peer, and societal modeling clearly plays a role as well. While well-adjusted youngsters can get tangled up in substance abuse, youngsters with other psychological or social problems are more substantially at risk.

The treatment of substance abuse is tiered: Inpatient treatment is the most intense, most structured level of care. It is appropriate for individuals whose use of substances is out of control, who need external imposition of sobriety and asylum from their usual drug-filled environment. Next is intensive outpatient treatment in which individuals live at home but attend treatment for several hours each day or evening. Finally, regular outpatient treatment involves meetings once to several times weekly, either of the self-help variety (A.A. or N.A.) or professionally led groups. Coexisting mental health problems may be treated concurrently or later, once stable sobriety has been achieved and a more accurate diagnosis can be made.

Group therapy is the core service in substance abuse treatment because it is felt that users are more adept at identifying and confronting each other's denial, rationalization, and excuses than are mental health professionals. In addition, group members who are more advanced in recovery can assist and serve as role models for newer members, who may have little belief in their ability to remain drug-free.

Family involvement in treatment is also standard, since substance abuse is considered a "family disease" in that family members find their own lives changed in profound ways by the individual's use pattern. They may unwittingly aid and abet the use by making excuses for the user and by covering up or bailing the user out of problems created by the use, or they may distance themselves from the user.

The prognosis for adolescent substance abuse and dependence is variable. In general, the better the underlying mental health, the more adequate the support system, the less the family history for substance abuse, and the later in life the abuse pattern begins, the better the prognosis.

The Developmental Perspective

Alcohol or drug use patterns develop gradually in youngsters, but abuse and dependence are extremely rare before adolescence. Why is adolescence a time of such particularly high risk for substance abuse? Addictions represent or compensate for major deficits in ego development and emotional states. That is, if youngsters have had disruptions in early life regarding relationships with others, they may be handicapped as they approach adolescence and its demands for sexual and emotional intimacy. Drug use can reduce painful emotional states, particularly the anxiety associated with intimacy. Youngsters who can't tolerate that anxiety may prefer to "numb out." In some cases, drug use can function as a substitute for intimacy. Drug using itself becomes the basis for interactions among peers and genuine intimacy is forgone. Youngsters who are particularly needy of social acceptance may be at increased risk. Adolescence is also the time of independence seeking and risk taking. The forbidden nature of drug use makes it more attractive to youngsters who have particularly strong needs to feel like adults.

Once drug use progresses to abuse, further development is seriously derailed. Motivation for non-drug activities is generally reduced. This means school attendance and work production will likely diminish. Friendship networks will shrink and change as substance abusers associate more and more with others who have the same objectives: procuring and using the substance of choice. Love and sexual relationships will be distorted by drug abuse. It is often said in A.A. that alcohol becomes the alcoholic's "best friend." No one else matters; anyone else can be betrayed for the sake of alcohol. Certainly the same is true for other drugs of abuse: Loyalty, attachment, and trust are all disrupted.

Unfortunately, once drug abuse or dependence is firmly established, relapse, even after successful treatment, is a constant threat. At this point, the individual has filled his or her life with drug-use cues, built psychological defenses that support drug use, developed social networks that revolve around drug-using behaviors, and found an artificial way to feel good no matter what the reality of life. In addition, if use began before or during adolescence, the individual may have had little experience building drug-free relationships or developing functional work or leisure habits. Thus, a thirty-year-old who achieves abstinence after fifteen years of drug abuse may have the psychological and social development of a fifteen-year old but the expectations of a thirty-year-old. This situation generates anxiety, which can fuel relapse. Therefore, repairing developmental delays and gaps is an integral part of the recovery process.

Questions to Consider

1. List all of the risk factors in Caitlin's case. Do you believe that any of them were necessary conditions for the development of drug abuse? Do you believe that any of them alone were sufficient conditions?

2. Psychotherapy rests on the principle of confidentiality. Generally, what a patient or client says to the therapist cannot be revealed to others without specific permission. Did Caitlin's therapist do the right thing by violating this principle in this case? Why or why not? What general guidelines make sense to you with respect to the privacy of communication between adolescent clients and therapists? Are these different from the guidelines you would advocate for child clients and for adult clients? How so?

3. *DSM* lists substance abuse and dependence as psychological "disorders." Recently, there has been great debate about whether addictions constitute genuine "illnesses." Should treatment of addictions be covered by medical insurance? Should addicts be protected under the Americans with Disabilities Act? Should drug users populate our jail cells? What is your view? Why?

4. Our society gives mixed messages about drugs. For example, the two substances that pose the greatest public health risk, nicotine and alcohol, are legal. What would constitute a coherent message about drug use? Do you think promulgation of this message through public education would be beneficial? Why or why not?

5. Consider your own friendship network. Do you have friends who engage in problematic substance use? How can you tell that they are substance abusers rather than users? What risk factors can you identify in their backgrounds or personalities that might have put them in harm's way? What psychological defenses do they exhibit to defend their substance use?

20

BULIMIA: THE CASE OF CORINNE D

CORINNE HAD BEEN a bright, engaging, active, and successful teenager, her parents reported, until now, the middle of her senior year in high school. She was an honor student, a varsity swimmer and soccer player, and photo editor of the yearbook. But lately she seemed listless and moody. She appeared to be having a hard time concentrating, and her grades had dropped, although not horribly. Even more alarming, her oft-stated intention to go away to college seemed to be wavering. Recently, she had wondered aloud whether she ought not to stay at home and get a job. Her self-confidence, they said, was nil.

Corinne was the older of two children. Her parents were both high school teachers. They had been married nineteen years, and they both described the marriage as a good one. Mrs. D's father and two of her uncles had been alcoholics, but there was no other history of emotional problems in either family. Mr. and Mrs. D seemed eager to cooperate in providing whatever information would be helpful in treating their daughter.

What Mr. and Mrs. D did not say, because they did not know, was that Corinne was bulimic. Several times a week, in guilt-ridden secrecy, she consumed huge quantities of food and then stuck her finger down her throat and vomited it all up. What do we mean by huge quantities? Try this: a half gallon of vanilla ice cream with a whole pecan pie, two large bags of potato chips, a bag of taco chips and a jar of salsa, a pound of chocolate-covered pretzels, four hot dogs in buns with some potato salad on the side, and two large glasses of coffee milkshake.

It had all started with a simple diet that Corinne went on over the summer. She had wanted to look good in a bathing suit. She knew her weight was "average" according to the charts, but she felt that her thighs, rear, and bust were all too big. She read fashion magazines and from them she knew how she was supposed to look—and she didn't look at all like that!

Corinne didn't have much patience, so the diet she chose was quite a severe one. Joined by her mother, who also wanted to lose some weight, she ate a grapefruit and a slice of dry toast in the morning, a salad with a squeeze of lemon at lunch, and a small square of chicken or fish with another salad at dinner. No snacks, no deviations. Mrs. D lasted four days, placidly returning to her previous style of eating before a week was up, but this only made Corinne more determined to succeed. However, watching her family eat breakfast and dinner stretched her self-control to the limit. She found herself thinking about food constantly, staring raptly at the food ads on television, reading the recipes written in the local newspaper.

By the second week, Corinne was having "slips," sneaking a candy bar here, a handful of chips there, a glass of Coke when no one was watching. Each slip filled her with self-disgust. Each time, she thought of herself as a "stupid hog" or a "pitiful incompetent" and vowed not to slip again. However, much to her dismay, just the opposite happened: The slips got bigger and bigger. One evening, after eating a candy bar, a large Coke, and a bag of nacho chips, Corinne felt so stuffed, so horrified, and so desperate that she ran to the bathroom and made herself throw up. It was difficult, and she had to stick her finger way down her throat over and over before she succeeded. After it was all over, dizzy, disgusted, but strangely calm, she staggered to bed. "Never again," she vowed, "I will never stuff myself like that again."

And yet she did. Knowing that she could rid herself of the calories by throwing up, Corinne's self-control gradually disappeared. She ate little in front of others, but alone at night, with food she had bought or "borrowed" from friends or the family's stores, she binged and purged. While she had managed to keep her eating behavior secret from her family, she had been unable to conceal its emotional sequelae: depression, preoccupation, self-hatred. By the time her parents brought her to therapy for her "depression," she was bingeing three to four times a week and had begun shoplifting food from stores to support her habit.

Corinne didn't directly tell her therapist that she was bulimic, but she must have been ready to deal with it, because shortly after therapy started, Mrs. D reported to the therapist that she had found herself awake one night and thought she heard Corinne gagging in the bathroom. She had gone to see what was wrong and had found the bathroom door locked. Corinne wouldn't let her in, saying that she was fine, she was just going to take a shower—and then the sound of water had drowned out any attempt at further conversation. The therapist chose to have Mrs. D discuss her fears with Corinne during the therapy hour, and Corinne confessed, with apparent relief, to the bingeing and vomiting.

Disclosing that she was bulimic was the beginning of a long, but hardly smooth road to recovery. At first, Corinne said that she could just stop. When the therapist reminded her that she had tried over and over to stop and might need some help, Corinne reluctantly agreed that continuing therapy might make sense. Over the next weeks, she and her therapist went over her eating journal, looking for emotional triggers of bingeing episodes, exploring her attitudes about eating and weight, and trying out alternative behaviors to use when she felt like bingeing. They discussed the goals she had set for herself and the fact that she couldn't tolerate not reaching them, even if some of them were unrealistically high. She seemed to think in all-or-nothing terms. For example, her recent thoughts about forgoing college had been based on worries that she might not be able to keep up her nearly perfect academic average there. Rather than accept the possibility of becoming a B student, she had opted not to try. Her therapist also encouraged Corinne to eat more nourishing meals with several planned snacks so that she would not become so ravenously hungry, setting herself up for a bingeing episode. However, Corinne felt unable to do this, since by now eating had become associated with failure and she felt she was already failing quite often enough.

Corinne continued to work in therapy, but her progress was being affected by her family's attempts to help her. Her parents had responded to their own anxiety about Corinne's problem by lecturing her, listening at the bathroom door, searching her room for junk food stashes while she was away at school, and grounding her when they caught her in a binge. These tactics, though well meant, backfired in a big way. Corinne and her parents began having loud, painful arguments that always ended with both Corinne and her mother in tears and her father locked in his study in stony silence. At these times, Corinne would balk at the whole process, denying that what she was doing was a problem and threatening to quit therapy. Throwing up was disgusting, sure, but it worked to keep her weight in line, and anyway it wasn't anybody's business. The therapist gently reminded Corinne of how she felt about herself and of how the eating disorder had consumed her life and robbed her of self-esteem. Corinne had no choice but to agree that this was true.

At this point, Corinne agreed to some family sessions so that everybody could sort out whose responsibility was what. These sessions, although sometimes stormy, helped Corinne's parents become clearer about what they could and couldn't control. They also talked together about how eating and weight were viewed in their family and in our culture. Mrs. D admitted that she had been struggling with her own weight for years and never seemed satisfied with how she looked. This led to a greater level of intimacy and trust between mother and daughter. Corinne, with the therapist's help, told her father how his compliments about her looks had always confused her. He complimented her brother on his grades and soccer prowess; he admired Corinne's hair and clothes. Gradually, the whole family's awareness of their (and our) gender-based biases and expectations increased.

Still, Corinne continued to binge and purge, although at a reduced frequency. The school year was coming to a close and Corinne decided to go off to college as she had originally planned, although she was concerned that her eating disorder would worsen under the added stress that college would inevitably bring. Her therapist contacted the counseling center at the college and found that they had an ongoing support group for students with eating disorders. They also agreed to assign her a counselor whom she would meet during her orientation week and who would see her as needed throughout her freshman year, at least. Armed with the knowledge that bulimia was more often controlled than "cured," Corinne went off to college with some anxiety but also with a feeling that she had a "safety net" in place, should she begin to fall back.

[This case is discussed along with the next case of an eating disorder on pages 152–156.]

21

ANOREXIA: THE CASE OF BARBARA B

THE PSYCHIATRIST who had evaluated Barbara described her as a "hap-less young woman." Her outpatient therapist, a psychologist to whom she had been referred for follow-up care after a twelve-day stay at an inpatient eating disorders program, characterized her as a "painfully shy, somber youngster." She had been hospitalized because of acute weight loss. Before that, Barbara, a twelve-year-old seventh-grader, had dieted for three months. During her diet, her preoccupation with her weight had increased, even as her size had decreased. She had eaten virtually nothing for the five days preceding her hospitalization.

Barbara was the younger of two children. Her brother, age nineteen, still lived at home. Both parents were employed and their marriage appeared to be stable and supportive. There was no apparent history of mental illness or substance abuse in the family, although Barbara's brother, Jason, was described as "emotional." Jason had had a school phobia in sixth grade, had difficulty maintaining relationships, and was moody and frequently angry. Apparently, Jason had harassed and bullied Barbara throughout their lives. The parents reported with chagrin that Jason had often focused on Barbara's weight (always well within the normal range), calling her "Tub" and "Lard Legs."

Barbara was described by her parents as having always been quite shy. She had quit singing in the chorus in fourth grade because she didn't like being in front of an audience. She had always wanted to run track but was afraid to try out for the team for fear of embarrassing herself by doing poorly. While otherwise a fairly good student, she was unable to read aloud in class or present oral assignments because of performance anxiety. Barbara had had one best friend from child-hood, but over the summer this friend had begun hanging out with a group of youngsters that ostracized Barbara and threatened to beat her up. This had left her bereft and totally isolated.

Despite having been discharged as "improved" from the hospital,

Barbara admitted to her therapist that she had merely complied with their rules to get out. She quickly resumed the goal of losing weight. She felt "huge" and had restricted her food intake to three or four "safe" items (primarily bagels with a thin smear of no-fat cream cheese). She continually weighed herself, sometimes a dozen times a day, and thought about food, eating, and her weight almost constantly.

Therapy was difficult for Barbara. She was not used to talking about her feelings. She seemed almost immobilized by suppressed rage at her brother—and at her parents for tolerating his behavior. She began tentatively voicing these feelings in sessions. However, between the third and fourth sessions, Barbara made some superficial cuts on her wrists. She explained to her therapist that she had not meant to kill herself, but the cutting had somehow relieved the tension she had been feeling. Together, they agreed that Barbara would keep careful track of the incidents and feelings that provoked the urge to cut and that she would try an alternative behavior—holding ice cubes tightly in her hands—when she felt like she just had to do something to reduce her distress.

Over the next several weeks, Barbara's weight continued to drop. Interestingly, she reported being noticeably hungry after therapy visits, which had been increased in frequency to twice a week. She had a couple of additional episodes of self-injury, always provoked by feeling angry and then guilty and frightened. Needless to say, her parents were becoming increasingly concerned at her apparent deterioration.

Finally, her pediatrician, who had been monitoring her physical condition on a weekly basis, noticed that Barbara seemed exceedingly weak. Laboratory tests indicated that her blood sugar and electrolytes were unstable. Barbara was transported to the hospital by ambulance and readmitted, this time to the adolescent psychiatry ward, since her parents felt that her stay in the eating disorders unit had been ineffective.

This time, hospitalization had the desired outcome. At first, Barbara responded as she had the last time; she obeyed the rules but participated minimally in ward activities. But then, after the second of two family therapy meetings, Barbara confessed privately to her mother that she had been sexually abused by an older female cousin numerous times over the course of about a year when she had been about eight years old. She had managed to forget about these incidents until her cousin's baby had been born, at which time she had started having intrusive images and memories related to the abuse. Barbara's parents reacted well. They responded with appropriate outrage for her, expressed their sadness that she had been hurt in this way, and affirmed their support for whatever way she chose to handle the situation from then on.

After this revelation, Barbara felt more ready to be discharged. Back at home, she resumed seeing her psychologist. Therapy included family sessions focused on helping Barbara and her family decide whether to confront the cousin, whether to tell the cousin's parents, whether to tell other family members, and whether to attend family events at which the cousin would be present. In all of these decisions, Barbara was allowed to take the lead, with her parents admirably supporting her choices, even when it was difficult for them.

In individual therapy sessions, Barbara worked through her feelings of shame and guilt about the incidents. She began to confront her sense of herself as damaged goods and the effects of this perception on her social behavior.

Because of the effects of the trauma on her self-perceptions, and because of her preexisting social anxiety, Barbara was reintroduced to the school milieu gradually after her return from the hospital. She began with home tutoring and then started attending school for half days after several months and full days at the beginning of the next school year. At the same time, therapy helped her to identify and practice specific social skills, including making eye contact, smiling, saying "hi," and beginning conversations with others. She and her therapist also worked on helping her accept that making mistakes, saying something foolish, and not being liked by someone were parts of life—not very enjoyable, but not catastrophes either. Gradually, and in a controlled way, she began to take some modest social risks.

Therapy continued for four more years, although at decreasing frequency over time. By the end, Barbara was meeting with her therapist only once every six weeks or so. She had gone through a period of heavy drinking at parties but had come through it unscathed. She had developed a small group of friends with whom she attended football games. She had had her first boyfriend and had used therapy to help her negotiate issues of intimacy and sexuality. Her weight and eating habits had stabilized. She had become a vegetarian and still ate a relatively low-fat diet, but within these constraints she ate a full range of foods, without much attention to her weight.

Living in the same household with her brother still sometimes drove Barbara to distraction, and she occasionally wondered if she might be better off living at her grandmother's house until she went to college. Jason had been unwilling to participate in therapy, and Mr. and Mrs. B felt that, because of his own psychological vulnerabilities, they had to offer Jason a safe place to live no matter how annoying his behavior. However, now that Barbara had a life of her own, she was at home less. She had also learned to stand up for herself and to throw back a few verbal barbs of her own on occasion. This made household life a bit less serene, but her parents understood that this was normal adolescent behavior. They felt that Barbara's mental health was well worth the price.

When it came time to terminate, Barbara and her family left treatment with the understanding that the rest of her adolescence, and perhaps her adult life as well, would present adaptive challenges for which therapy might be useful. They knew that coming back for help, should Barbara begin to have difficulties in the future, would not be a sign of failure but a sign of strength.

Thinking about the Cases

Anorexia nervosa, the "relentless pursuit of thinness," and its cousin, bulimia, the binge-purge syndrome, are dangerous disorders that can lead to emaciation, loss of menstruation, decreases in bone density, severe tooth decay, drops in blood pressure, anemia, cardiac arrhythmias, and even death. While it is exceedingly rare for males to develop eating disorders, anorexia affects approximately 1 percent of females in Western cultures and bulimia affects another 1 percent (although eating binges are reported in as many as 30 percent of college-age women). Interestingly, eating disorders are diseases "of plenty," with an exceedingly small incidence in poor countries.

Eating disorders tend to begin between the ages of twelve and twenty-five. Sometimes triggered by "normal" dieting, by illness which is accompanied by weight loss, or in response to an environmental stressor of some sort (boyfriend, family, or school problems), the young woman becomes preoccupied with losing weight. In anorexia, body image becomes increasingly distorted, with anorexics often describing, as Barbara did, feeling fatter and fatter as their weight decreases. While some anorexics simply restrict their food intake, others exercise excessively or use vomiting, laxatives, or diuretics to purge what little they have eaten. Bulimics may also use these methods but in the service of maintaining their weight in the face of binges rather than in the service of continual weight loss.

Eating disorders often co-occur with a host of other psychological problems including personality disorders, anxiety and mood disorders, post-traumatic stress disorders, somatization disorders, and substance abuse disorders. Barbara clearly had a preexisting social anxiety disorder as well as some symptoms of post-traumatic stress disorder. She may even have been clinically depressed at the beginning of treatment. Corinne, on the other hand, did not appear to have any other mental health diagnoses.

Like most other disorders, eating disorders are multidetermined. Biological predispositions to mood disorder may be relevant in anorexics. In fact, mood disorders often accompany anorexia and are found with increased frequency in the family members of individuals with anorexia. Bulimia often occurs in families with histories of alcoholism, like Corinne's, and alcoholism may co-occur with or supplant bulimia in individual instances. Further, disturbed hypothalamic functioning accompanies anorexia, but it is not known yet whether this is cause or effect of self-starvation. Temperamental traits like social sensitivity and a tendency toward rigidity or perfectionism, apparent in both Corinne's and Barbara's cases, may also be relevant.

Cultural norms dictating that the ideal body shape is ultra-thin no doubt also play a role. Young women who are slightly heavy or who enter puberty earlier may be more vulnerable to poor body image based on insistent societal messages and may succumb to the pressure by going on extremely restrictive diets that set the stage for either bulimia or anorexia.

Of course, psychological factors are also implicated. It has been observed, for example, that starving makes young women with anorexia feel powerful and in control, whereas eating makes them feel weak and anxious. Psychological theories about anorexia expand on this observation, hypothesizing that environmental conditions or events that interfere with the normal development of autonomy would predispose a young woman to anorexia. These might include having overcontrolling parents or, like Barbara, a history of trauma in which she felt powerless to protect herself. Physical abuse and sexual abuse are, in fact, fairly prevalent in the histories of many anorexics. Note that Barbara also felt powerless to protect herself from her brother's taunts or to attract and keep friends.

Treatment for eating disorders is also multidimensional. Sometimes antidepressant medication can be helpful, particularly in reducing the urge to binge in bulimics, but psychotherapy of one sort or another is necessary. Cognitive therapy can help to correct unrealistic beliefs about eating and weight control. It can also help to change dysfunctional attitudes about oneself and others. Behavioral therapy, including relaxation training and the kind of skills training that Barbara engaged in, is often used as well. Interpersonal psychotherapy focuses on helping the young woman understand, confront, and manage conflicts with others more successfully. Supportive and psychodynamic psychotherapy can improve self-image and resistance to stress. Family therapy may also play a role, particularly when the patient is a young adolescent or when parental behavior is specifically at issue, as it was with Corinne's family. Even when it is not, as in Barbara's case, consultation with the parents to help them understand and manage their daughter's disorder is essential as the anorexia greatly increases stress and distress in families. Group treatment is sometimes attempted, although it is tricky: Anorexic girls have a tendency to compete with each other to see who can lose the most weight!

Hospitalization plays a role in the treatment of anorexia and, more rarely, bulimia. Sometimes patients need to be medically stabilized and forced to ingest enough calories to sustain life. As a last resort, tube feeding may be used, but more often a system of gaining and losing privileges to move about freely on the ward (another form of behavioral therapy) is used to encourage normal eating. As you can imagine, if autonomy is truly a central issue in anorexia, forced hospitalization and forced eating are to be avoided if at all possible.

Because anorexics and bulimics often do not see anything wrong with their behavior, treatment is difficult and can take a long time. The outcome is variable. Death is a very real risk in anorexia, with the rate of mortality being approximately 15 percent. The risk is less in bulimia, but severe bingeing and purging can cause acute disturbances in electrolyte balance that may lead to cardiac abnormalities and death. The best predictor of a positive response to treatment is proximity to normal body weight. Thus, in general, bulimics have the best prognosis and severely ill anorexics the worst. In addition, the earlier in the course of the disorder that treatment is instituted, the better.

Those sufferers who survive often continue to struggle with eating and weight for many years, generally doing better when their lives are calm and worse when stresses occur. Some, like Barbara, recover substantially. For her, the appropriate support of her family, the working through of the underlying trauma, and the availability of long-term psychotherapy all contributed to her good outcome. However, many others are like Corinne, whose inconsistent insight and motivation, perfectionism, secrecy, and extreme vulnerability to how others see her make the prognosis for the future guarded.

The Developmental Perspective

It is no accident that eating disorders develop most often during adolescence and very early adulthood. To the extent that cultural expectations for thinness are involved, these tend to impinge more and more as girls make the transition from childhood to adulthood. At this stage of life, it is developmentally appropriate for the locus of emotional reward to shift from parents to peers. Youngsters typically become exquisitely sensitive to what other youngsters think of them. They can spend hours a day staring at themselves in a mirror, examining their face, hair, physique, and dress. For girls, in particular, beauty (rather than skills or accomplishments) is still the prime currency. Popularity is a harsh master, and thin girls have an edge over those who are not.

In addition, issues of autonomy become paramount in adolescence. In healthy households, parental rules gradually give way to independent decision making as youngsters appear more and more capable of making good choices. In these households flexible parents expect their children to make some mistakes and to learn from them. However, when parents are unable to tolerate errors from their children or feel an overwhelming need to protect them from pain or risk, youngsters may be inhibited in learning life skills and in developing healthy self-confidence. An unsuccessful or difficult transition from the helplessness of childhood to the independence of adulthood can precipitate anorexic behavior in vulnerable girls.

Self-control is first cousin to autonomy, as bulimia is to anorexia. Adolescence is also the time when a variety of tempting but self-destructive options become more available: promiscuous sex, drugs, and food choices among them. While parents exert control over youngsters, adolescents must learn to exert control over themselves. Bulimia can be seen as an indicator of difficulty in mastering this important developmental task.

Adolescence is also a time when dyadic sexual behavior becomes a possibility. Our culture sends very mixed messages to girls about sexuality: Sex before marriage is now commonly accepted, girls are becoming sexually active at younger and younger ages, and most girls experience moderate to severe anxiety about when and under what circumstances to "do it." Yet society also encourages girls to be attractive and sexually alluring. For some, anorexia may be a convenient way out from the relentless pressure to make decisions about sexuality. Starving can interfere with menstruation and will certainly make the body look relatively prepubescent. Looking like a child can stave off, at least to some extent, the stresses of being a woman.

Finally, eating disorders, once established, derail normal development even further. Girls who are preoccupied with weight and eating behavior tend to become self-centered and even more introverted than they were before. They lose interest in and energy for outside activities and thus have less and less in common with their peers. They often perceive themselves to be on a quest that no one else can comprehend. The inevitable guilt and shame that accompany the persistent sense of both abnormality and failure experienced by these young women preclude the development of healthy self-esteem. The normal developmental tasks of developing a flexible adult self-image that includes many roles and interests and learning to relate intimately to others may be accomplished only incompletely or not at all.

Questions to Consider

1. Eating disorders have been characterized as addictions by some researchers and clinicians. What are the similarities between an eating disorder and, say, alcoholism? What are the differences?

2. Consider your own attitude toward your weight, the weight of others, and eating behaviors. Do you consider it "healthy"? Why or why not?

3. If you had a friend with an eating disorder (and many of you do), how would you try to help? Would you talk with her about it or ignore it? Would you tell her parents? Why or why not?

4. The data suggest that young women of African-American heritage have fewer eating disorders than Causasian or Asian-American young women. What are some reasons that this might be so?

5. If you wanted to inoculate a child against the possibility of developing an eating disorder as an adolescent, how might you do it? How confident would you be in the results of your intervention(s)?

PART SIX

Disorders of Emerging Identity

————◄○►————

W ho am I? For each of us, the answer to this question emerges gradually over the course of our lifetime. Some things we know early: I'm a boy or a girl; I'm a member of my particular family. Other things we learn in school: I enjoy studying or I have trouble with academics; I'm shy or I'm popular; I can play music or I'm good at sports. Yet other things we learn as we interact with our families and peers: I'm trustworthy or I'm dishonest; I'm timid or I'm a risk taker; I'm heterosexual or I'm homosexual. By adulthood, most of us form a reasonably coherent identity. We can describe ourselves to others (and to ourselves) in a comprehensible way.

For some people, this road to identity gets blocked or detoured. In this section, we consider three cases in which this happened. In the first, a little boy identifies himself as a girl so strongly that he insists on wearing girls' clothing and engaging in what are traditionally girls' activities. While cases like his are relatively rare, they do raise some fascinating questions about the biological and social aspects of the development of sexual identity. In the second case, a traumatized teenager represses the memory of the trauma so that her identity is split into the girl who knows what happened and the girl who does not. While her case illustrates a fairly mild and time-limited form of dissociative disorder, more severe cases, including multiple personality disorder, can markedly impair an individual's long-term functioning. The final case in this section is that of a youngster with borderline personality disorder, a severe and persistent disorder of identity, affectivity, relatedness, and impulse control. Personality disorders, as a group, are apparent by early adolescence and tend to persist throughout adulthood, although the most florid symptoms tend to diminish in middle age. While the *DSM* has separate categories for gender identity disorders, dissociative disorders, and personality disorders, we have grouped them together here because they all have to do with questions of identity.

22

GENDER IDENTITY DISORDER:
THE CASE OF BILLY B

BILLY WAS THE middle of three boys. He looked like his brothers—fair-skinned, blue-eyed, stocky boys—but there the resemblance ended. Although a variety of toys were available to him, Billy, from as early as his parents can remember, ignored the trucks and cars, guns and hammers, in favor of dolls. While his older brother went flying around the house, dressed as an "Indian" and whooping it up, Billy, at two and a half, sat quietly in a corner dressing and feeding one of his "babies." He eschewed rough-and-tumble play, preferring instead to follow his mother around while she went about her household routine. She also found him to be especially "sensitive" and in need of more gentle disciplining than her other sons. He would burst into tears at a harsh word from her and rarely needed the "time-out" punishments that seemed a part of daily life with his brothers.

By three and a half, Billy had started his own collection of dolls. His only playmate was a cousin who lived nearby, a girl of about the same age as he. Arriving at her house, he would run directly to her bedroom and spend the next several hours trying on all of her clothes. Together they would produce a "fashion show" for whatever parent was around, with Billy wearing his cousin's clothes while she wore her mother's. Like most children, Billy and his cousin spent a lot of time in fantasy play, but he always insisted on being a girl in their role playing. Sometimes they would argue about who got to be the "princess." Her suggestions that he could play the part of the "prince" were met with stony resistance.

His aunt found the obsessive, driven quality of his behavior disturbing, commenting, "It's as if he were possessed by the desire to try on every dress." His parents didn't know what to think. His mother was worried about his preference for traditionally feminine types of play, but her gentle attempts to redirect him were met with strong resistance or even tantrums. Motivated to raise nonsexist children in an atmosphere that downplayed traditional gender roles, she was hesitant to stifle his natural proclivities or damage his self-esteem by excessive criticism. When Billy asked her, as he often did while parading around in his cousin's clothes, "Don't I look pretty?" she would tell him, with much misgiving, that he did, indeed.

His father was much more upset by Billy's single-minded interest in things feminine. After a period of denial, he became increasingly agitated in Billy's presence, alternating between ignoring him and screaming at him to "knock it off and act like a boy." He tried spending more time alone with Billy doing "guy stuff," but these outings were usually disappointing for both father and son. In the toy store, Billy wanted to look at doll outfits and his father wanted to look at the sports section. Billy was bored and distracted playing catch and when his dad asked what he'd like to do next, he invited his father to a tea party. Mr. B tried to participate in his son's play, but it made him uncomfortable and frustrated.

A real parenting challenge came when Billy began to refuse to take off his cousin's clothes when it was time to return home. He threw such a fit that his mother, to calm his obviously real and palpable distress, finally let him wear the dress home, where he wore it all evening, much to his father's consternation, and insisted on going to bed in it that night. After several months of constant battling and anguish, Mrs. B, over her husband's vociferous objections, bought Billy his own dress. This did not end their struggles, however, since Billy also wanted to wear barrettes in his hair, his cousin's shoes (which were too small and hurt his feet), and her underwear.

By the age of five, Billy was voicing the clear wish to be a girl. At his fifth birthday party he told his mother, "I always thought that when I was this many [holding up five fingers] I would like being a boy, but I don't." She had observed him many times standing in front of the mirror exclaiming that he was ugly but that when he grew up he was "gonna be a pretty lady." He had no boy friends in nursery school, but the girls liked him just fine. He fit right into their play, and they treated him as if he were one of them.

At the time he entered school, his parents made several changes. First, they set limits on his cross-dressing. He was allowed to wear a girl's nightshirt and tights to bed and to wear girls' slippers, but otherwise he had to dress in boys' clothes. His mom and her sister agreed that the children would be allowed to dress in adults' clothes for "dress-up" but that Billy would no longer be allowed to wear his cousin's clothes. In fact, her bedroom was off-limits.

In addition, Mr. and Mrs. B enrolled Billy in a local ballet class that was run by a husband-and-wife team. They felt that this might give him a socially appropriate outlet for his feminine interests. They also hoped that the male ballet teacher would offer Billy a model for how to integrate the masculine and feminine sides of himself. Billy loved ballet and didn't seem to mind at all being the only boy in the class. He did throw a bit of a fit when the other students got to wear tutus and he didn't, but he seemed to get past this and settle into the class well.

Finally, at the urging of her sister, Billy's mother agreed to have him evaluated by a child psychiatrist. The psychiatrist saw Billy alone for several sessions, took a family and personal history from his parents, and saw the family together. She confirmed Billy's parents' fears: Billy had the identity of a girl in a boy's body. She called this "transsexualism."

Mrs. B was devastated. With a family history of depression and alcoholism, she felt that she herself had been raised "in the original dysfunctional family." She had had problems with depression throughout her own life and was primed and ready to believe that Billy's problems were somehow her fault.

The psychiatrist worked with Billy in individual therapy on a weekly basis for about a year. Therapy failed to produce any profound changes, although Billy seemed to accept limits on his cross-dressing with a great deal less struggle as time went on.

Mr. and Mrs. B, however, benefited greatly from their contacts with the psychiatrist. Mr. B moved past his anger and frustration to sadness and resignation. In doing so, he was more able to accept Billy as he was, rather than as he wished him to be. Mrs. B was able to overcome her guilty feelings enough to set better limits for Billy and to actively engage in problem solving with her husband about how to best help Billy cope with the social effects of his condition. Both came to view the situation as "an act of God" that must be accepted with grace and forbearance.

In kindergarten and first grade Billy did well academically and behaved in a way that did not get him singled out for ridicule by his classmates, although he had no real friends. Throughout elementary school, he continued to play with his dolls and avoided more typical "boy" activities. Gradually, this became more and more a problem with his peers and their families. Perhaps as a substitute, Billy developed an interest in computers, which occupied much of his free time and also provided a conduit to a more normal relationship with his father. Together they explored the Internet and played computer games.

At home and throughout his extended family, Billy's gender cross-identification became somewhat of a non-issue. "Bill is just Bill," his parents would say. They learned from their consultations with the psychiatrist and from their own reading on the subject that he was unlikely to change. They assumed that he will be homosexual as an adult and have prepared themselves to love and accept him regardless. They worry about what will become of him when he falls upon the rocky shores of adolescence, but they have resolved to approach problems as they arise, one day at a time.

Thinking about the Case

Gender identity disorder, also known as transsexualism, is diagnosed in individuals who feel trapped in a body of the wrong gender. It is a rare disorder, occurring in about 1 in 100,000 people. It is distinguishable from transvestism, in which clothing of the opposite sex is worn for erotic or playful reasons but in which the individual is fully identified with his or her own gender. Nor is it synonymous with homosexuality. While most transsexuals are sexually attracted to members of their own gender, some are not.

Billy's case is quite typical in that the disorder appears startlingly early, with fixed cross-gender identification in place by the age of three or four. It is diagnosed much more often in males than in females, although it should be noted that cross-dressing and other cross-gender behaviors are more socially acceptable for women than for men, so perhaps there are many undiagnosed cases. The presumed cause of gender identity disorder is some sort of abnormal hormonal condition in utero. It is a chronic condition, showing minimal change as a result of psychotherapy or behavioral therapy.

Until recently, despair was the certain future for those afflicted. However, within the past several decades, advances in medical knowledge and techniques have made the possibility of sex reassignment through hormonal and surgical procedures a viable alternative. Typically, an individual who wishes to have the surgery is required to undergo a careful psychological evaluation to ensure that the apparent gender identity disorder is not secondary to another disorder (such as schizophrenia). The psychological health and resilience of the person are also assessed. Then he or she is required to live in the new gender role for a period of several years while hormone therapy is begun. This may entail a change of name, dress, and sometimes even occupation. Finally, genital surgery and hormone treatment are undertaken. For male to female sex reassignment, this involves transforming the penis into a vagina. For female to male reassignment, the procedure is more complicated and involves multiple surgeries over several years to remove the breasts and ovaries and, sometimes, to build a penis. Since the penis cannot become erect, a prosthetic device must be used for intercourse.

The outcome of sex reassignment surgery is variable. Probably half or more of patients have a favorable outcome, reporting improvement in their sense of well-being and overall satisfaction with life. However, a substantial minority experience fairly serious surgical complications or feel that their lives have been altered in negative ways. Perhaps it will be possible some day to identify and correct the presumed fetal hormonal disturbance so that gender identity disorder can be prevented.

The Developmental Perspective

The early onset and immutable nature of gender identity disorder have led investigators to conclude that a hormonal disturbance that occurs some time in the second to fourth months of pregnancy is responsible for this fascinating but heartbreaking condition. In the early fetus, both male and female internal organs are present until, in male fetuses, two masculinizing hormones are secreted from the testes. These hormones affect the subsequent development of sexual organs and they have psychological effects on the brain—in effect, masculinizing the brain. In transsexuals, it appears that, for as-yet-unknown reasons, organ development proceeds normally but the masculinizing of the brain does not. While familial and social factors also play a role in the development of sexual identity, these later influences appear to reinforce or disturb a core identity that is established well before birth.

It is difficult to overstate the anguish felt by transsexuals as the social effects of their identification with the opposite gender develop over time. Billy did fine in the early school years, accepted by the girls and left alone by the boys. But by second or third grade, teasing and isolation began to grind away at his self-esteem. Many youngsters become profoundly depressed and even suicidal. Some, as adolescents or young adults, mutilate their own genitals. Almost always, disturbances of personality develop as they try to adapt to the demands and the stigma to which they are subject from an early age. While some succeed in developing the flamboyantly deviant self-identity of a transvestite drag queen, they pay a price: a deviant peer group, lack of spouse and family, disconnection from society. On the other hand, those who choose not to "come out" live a constricted life of quiet misery.

Questions to Consider

1. How might you, as a parent, help a child like Billy to become a psychologically healthy adult? What practical steps might you take?

2. Close your eyes and imagine, for a few minutes, what it would be like to be forced to wear the clothing of and to act like a member of the opposite sex. If you feel really courageous, try it for a day. What changes occurred in your mood, self-esteem, and ability to engage in everyday tasks and relate to others? What might it be like to have this be your permanent lot in life?

3. As we move from sexual identity through sexual orientation, sexual interest, and sexual behavior we appear to move along a continuum from biological to environmental/experiential influences. Can you construct a coherent biopsychosocial model that describes the development of adult sexuality?

4. Family systems theory often focuses on the effects of parental behavior on children. But children's behavior can also affect the family system. How do you suppose Billy's disorder might affect an otherwise "normal" family?

23

DISSOCIATIVE DISORDER:
THE CASE OF JESSIE P

JESSIE WAS A thin, fragile-looking fourteen-year-old when I first met her. With her red hair, freckles, and turned-up nose, she looked like she ought to have been far merrier than she was. Instead, she sat rigidly between her mother and stepfather on my office couch, eyes down, barely breathing. Two days earlier, she had been found, dirty and dazed, wandering the streets of a city more than eighty miles from her small New England hometown. She had been missing from home for four days by the time she turned up. Stranger still, she apparently couldn't recall when or why she had left home, how she had ended up so far away, or what had transpired in the four days. She knew who she was and where she lived, but she had not attempted to contact her frantic mother or to return home. She denied having run away, and she didn't think she had been abducted. She had absolutely no idea what had happened.

When she returned home, Jessie's family physician referred her to me for evaluation and treatment of her amnesia. She was accompanied to her first session by her mother and stepfather, both of whom had taken time off from work to bring her in. She also had an older brother, but he was in school.

Her parents described Jessie as a bright and charming youngster who was a good student, had lots of friends, and was planning a career in modeling. She had rarely been moody or difficult, although there had been some conflicts lately about her wanting to date. Her parents thought she was too young for single dating, but there was a guy she liked who had asked her to go to the movies with him. She had initially balked at their insistence that she go with a group of friends but had seemed to accept their decision after a bit.

Jessie's family history yielded some possibly relevant information.

Her parents had separated when she was five years old. At the time of the separation she had seemed fine emotionally, but she had developed a prolonged case of hives, which came each evening for about six months then gradually faded away as mysteriously as they had come. Her father had moved away, but she and her older brother saw him at holidays and in the summer. Her relationship with him seemed cordial if somewhat distant.

When Jessie was eight, her mother had remarried. Both of the children had been delighted because their new stepfather was an affable man who seemed to like spending time with them. He supported both children's interests, encouraging her brother in sports and Jessie in modeling. He often took their side when they got into disagreements with their mom about chores and rules. Jessie said he seemed like a big kid himself.

I was struck by an incongruity in Jessie's presentation. The words she used in talking about her stepfather were very positive, but the tone of her voice when she spoke about him was totally flat and her body seemed to shrink into itself. He talked a good deal about Jessie's modeling and about how he thought she could really make a go of it, with her fresh good looks and her thin figure. She had already made some money modeling for a local department store, and he had started helping her build a portfolio of photographs with which to attract an agent. Jessie's mom beamed while he spoke and remarked that she was lucky that she had found someone who was so good to her children.

At the end of the first session, I arranged for a series of individual visits with Jessie and, on a hunch, made sure that they occurred at times when only her mother could transport her to my office. For the first several visits, I just let Jessie get comfortable with me. I inquired about her friends, about school, about her boyfriend, and about her various interests. Interestingly, Jessie never mentioned modeling and, when I brought it up in the fifth visit, she winced. I noted aloud that the topic seemed to be uncomfortable for her and, while she denied it, she became, if anything, more wary and withdrawn. Quietly I explained that when a person had an episode of amnesia like she'd had, generally they had been severely upset or frightened by something that seemed so huge that it couldn't be managed. The mind acted to protect the person by "turning off." If the frightening thing were now gone, then maybe the mind wouldn't have to play any more tricks, but if it were still around, then it had to be faced consciously at some point so that a real rather than a "trick" solution could be found. I assured her that if she were to have the courage to face what had scared her, I would help her seek a solution as best I could. Jessie listened gravely to this small speech and then changed the subject.

Several more weeks went by and Jessie gradually began to speak spontaneously of modeling. She seemed to have mixed feelings about it, both enjoying and distrusting the attention it brought her. She wished that her stepfather would let it alone—he seemed more excited by her prospects than she was. She particularly disliked his taking pictures of her. She didn't know why—it just made her uncomfortable.

While I had asked Jessie several times about the events immediately preceding her disappearance, it wasn't until her fifteenth visit that she suddenly remembered that her stepfather had been doing a "photo shoot" that day. The memory actually came as a vision or flashback of herself in underwear posing in the bedroom. Visibly distraught, shaking and hyperventilating, Jessie had to be reassured and calmed down before she could describe what she had "seen." She reported that her stepfather had taken a series of pictures of her in various stages of undress: in panties and bra, in a nylon nightgown, in panties alone. He had had her pose leaning up against the bed and lying on the bed in suggestive postures. He had reassured her repeatedly that his interest in her was purely professional, that the pictures were necessary for her portfolio. After all, hadn't she seen partially nude photos in numerous fashion advertisements in her modeling magazines? At last, he had photographed her nude in the shower and had left her there to finish washing her hair and go to bed. She did, indeed, go to bed, but a few hours later, in the middle of the night, she arose. Having forgotten the incident of the previous day, but feeling dazed and frightened, Jessie took all of her savings from her underwear drawer and left the house. She walked to the bus station and went as far as her money would take her. For the next several days she had literally lived on the street, foraging for food in trash cans and sleeping in the park with the rest of the homeless and forgotten. The fact that she hadn't been assaulted constituted a bona fide miracle.

Jessie's confession put me in a quandary. She, naturally, couldn't bear the thought of telling anyone else about what had happened. She felt sure that it would tear her family apart—if her mother even believed her at all. She could hardly believe, herself, that what she had told me had really happened. It still seemed like a dream. Besides, she loved her stepfather and didn't want to hurt him. Nonetheless, I firmly told her that her safety was my first priority and that I couldn't let her return to a home that felt dangerous to her. She and I had to take some steps to protect her.

The next half hour was one of the toughest I've ever had. We called Jessie's mother into the room and Jessie told her story. Her mother was shocked but not disbelieving. She burst into tears and hugged her daughter, who was also crying. Then both of them looked at me. What now?

Together we made a plan. Jessie would spend the night (and perhaps the next few nights) at her best friend's house. Jessie's mom and stepdad would come in together the next day for an emergency session. Jessie's mom felt that she could hold off on confronting him until then, and she wanted to have my assistance when she did.

What a relief it was that Jessie's stepfather didn't deny what Jessie had described. He did, however, insist for a while that what he had done wasn't wrong. He had been raised in a family in which people walked around nude in front of each other, and he didn't see the problem, he said. As we continued to talk, his defensiveness was gradually battered by my insistence that he look at how his behavior had affected Jessie. To his credit, he finally broke down and tearfully apologized to his wife, saying that he'd not meant to cause any harm, that he loved her and the children, and that he would do anything, including getting ongoing counseling for himself, to keep the family together.

As a mental health professional, I was mandated to report incidents of suspected child abuse or neglect to the local social services department. I suggested that we do this together, feeling fairly sure that we could develop a satisfactory plan that would provide for Jessie's safety and that might, if all went well, allow the family to remain together. The elements of this plan were that Jessie's stepfather would apologize to her and that, with her mother present, he would encourage Jessie to tell him and report to her mother if he did anything that made her feel uncomfortable. He assured her that there would be no more photos, clothed or otherwise, and that he would respect her privacy in her room and in the bathroom.

Counseling for this family continued for close to a year. The therapist worked sometimes with all three together, sometimes with a pair of family members, and sometimes with one member alone. Mr. P needed to work on admitting and understanding why he had breached appropriate boundaries with Jessie. He and Mrs. P had work to do to repair their relationship. In the process, they learned to communicate more honestly. It took some time for Jessie to feel safe with her stepfather again, but his genuine contrition and patient tolerance for her ambivalence paid off in the long run.

Thinking about the Case

Dissociative disorders involve a disruption in the functions of consciousness, memory, identity, or perception of the environment. These disruptions appear to occur in response to a massive, seemingly unresolvable conflict. They are called "dissociative" because two or more mental processes that are usually integrated become disconnected.

The most notorious dissociative disorder is multiple personality disorder (MPD), in which various separate and distinct personalities reside within one person, alternating control of the individual's behavior and often having no awareness that the other personalities exist. Patients with this disorder tend to come into treatment complaining of memory lapses or headaches or unexplainable behavior of some sort. The MPD is then "discovered" in the therapy process. While the press has reported on cases in which dozens or even hundreds of personalities have been claimed by patients, there is a great deal of controversy in professional circles about MPD. Some researchers assert that MPD is underdiagnosed, whereas others suggest that it is extremely rare and most of the cases reported are fakes. The existence of dissociation itself, however, is not in question.

While amnesia, a dissociative process in which certain memories are split off from consciousness, can result from physical causes, such as a blow to the head, alcoholism, Alzheimer's disease, or stroke, it can also result from extreme stress or unresolvable conflict. Jessie experienced a classic psychogenic amnesia and fugue (which means "flight"). In Jessie's case, the conflict revolved around responding to and managing the feelings caused by her stepfather's boundary-violating behavior. On the one hand, since he was behaving as if everything was fine and since she loved and wanted to please him (and her mother, who also loved him), she could not voice her extreme discomfort. On the other hand, she was unable to quell the feelings of fear and guilt that the picture taking evoked. She could neither trust and act on her feelings nor ignore them—a classic "no-win" situation that typically results in extreme anxiety. Consciously fleeing would not solve the situation, since it would be tantamount to admitting to her feelings. But "forgetting" what had happened and fleeing the situation—now that was another story.

Dissociative disorders and their close relatives, conversion disorders (psychogenic blindness, deafness, paralysis, or muscle weakness), were quite common ways of coping with emotional stress in the days of Sigmund Freud, whose experiences with these patients led him to hypothesize the existence of the "unconscious" mind. They are also found with some frequency in wartime situations in which fighting can be virtually suicidal and running away is not allowed. In peacetime, however, these disorders are fairly rare in our culture, probably partly because our medical diagnostic techniques have become so sophisticated that physical causes can generally be ruled out quite readily.

In treating dissociative or conversion disorders, the therapist may be forced to assume the role of detective, trying to uncover the unconscious conflict or traumatic event that precipitated the symptoms. This may involve no more than developing a trusting relationship and undertaking a painstaking examination of the known facts, as in Jessie's case. Memory losses sometimes resolve spontaneously over a few days' or weeks' time. In some cases, simply suggesting, in a confident manner, that the memories will return speeds the process. Occasionally, hypnosis is used as an adjunct to treatment. When it is, however, great care is required since it is quite possible for people to fabricate stories under hypnosis. This is particularly true for highly suggestible people, and research indicates that individuals who develop dissociative or conversion disorders are, indeed, strongly suggestible.

The Developmental Perspective

Since dissociative disorders in children have not been the focus of a great deal of research, little is known about the developmental aspects. Some data suggest that multiple personality disorder often occurs because of trauma that afflicts a child who is between the ages of four and six.

Dissociation as a process is quite common in younger children. Preschoolers engage in a great deal of fantasy play, often with imaginary playmates. On a scale of childhood dissociative behavior, younger children score higher, with scores gradually declining and then disappearing at around nine or ten years of age. There is some evidence that children whose scores do not decline with age are predisposed to psychopathology. Youngsters with abnormally high scores tend to have a variety of psychiatric diagnoses, and sexually abused girls score higher than average for their age.

The effects of abnormal dissociation on development can be profound. A youngster who develops an early and persistent dissociative response to stress may have difficulty with everyday tasks like learning in school and developing friendships. Other youngsters may see her behavior and ways of relating as disturbing or perplexing. If the dissociation begins early enough, the development of a secure sense of attachment may be impaired. Later on, it will be difficult for a coherent sense of identity to develop. Clearly, the earlier the trauma and the more pervasive the dissociative response, the more normal development will be derailed. When the trauma occurs after many developmental tasks have been accomplished, as in Jessie's case, less damage may occur.

Questions to Consider

1. Not all cases of sexual abuse (or milder boundary violations) within the family go as well as this one did. What do you think are some of the factors that led to the good outcome? How many of these were under the therapist's control?

2. Some therapists would insist that Mr. and Mrs. P separate for Jessie's welfare. How do you imagine that staying together as a family might affect Jessie's adolescent and young adult development? How might marital separation and divorce have affected her? What are some of the factors that would help a family decide what is the right thing to do?

3. Why do you suppose some people develop dissociative reactions to stress and conflict while others don't? Can you develop a study or experiment that would allow you to test your hypotheses?

24

BORDERLINE PERSONALITY DISORDER: THE CASE OF APRIL S

APRIL AND HER SISTER, May, came into the office together and sat down next to each other on the sofa. While the family resemblance was apparent, the differences in presentation were striking. May was just sixteen, a wholesome-looking teenager with clean, shoulder-length blond hair, wearing a "preppy" color-coordinated outfit. She sat upright, looking anxious and subdued but eager to please. April, on the other hand, was a wary-looking thirteen-year-old who affected a "punk" style. Her hair was cut raggedly and dyed several colors of yellow and orange. She wore a huge black workshirt, oversized floppy jeans, and black boots. Both girls were referred for therapy by their family physician with the goal of helping to ameliorate the psychological effects of a particularly chaotic and pernicious family situation.

The girls' parents had been divorced for many years. Both parents had had severe problems with alcohol and, while their father had been sober for five years and had remarried an apparently healthy woman, their mother continued to drink heavily and use other drugs, including marijuana and cocaine. She had remained single but had had numerous liaisons, producing additional children along the way. The girls had two younger half-brothers on their mother's side and a half-sister on their father's side. At the time of intake, they were both living at their father's and stepmother's. May had voluntarily gone there about a year earlier, and April had just recently joined them after a violent argument with her mother.

The girls' family life had been remarkable for its instability and inconstancy. Their parents' marriage had been marked by frequent loud arguments in which crockery, and sometimes knives, got thrown. After their parents split up, their mother, who had retained custody of them by default, hooked up with another drug abuser whom the girls described as "a real jerk." The family moved back and forth from this man's house to their grandmother's whenever he and their mother had a fight, which occurred "at least fifteen times." The girls said that their mother "fought with everybody" and couldn't stay in any relationship for very long. During one argument one of her later boyfriends stabbed himself with a knife—both girls had watched the whole scene from a doorway. Ironically, this was the boyfriend that the girls had felt the most comfortable with, even though they thought he was "mental."

May reported having had much of the responsibility for April's upbringing. Beginning by the time May was four, their mother had, from time to time, left the children alone for days at a time without food or supervision. She also took them to the bar with her, often getting so drunk that she passed out in the bathroom or on the street. At these times, May would call their father, who, if she could find him, would come and take them to his home overnight until their mother sobered up. Sometimes, their mother's mother would come to the rescue. Other times, May just coped on her own, tending to April's needs as well as, after a while, the new baby's. While the girls denied sexual abuse, they admitted that their mother often slapped or tried to strangle them when she was drunk, stoned, and angry. In addition, they reported, she had virtually ruined their social relationships, embarrassing them in front of their friends, crashing school parties to dance, drunk, with their boyfriends, and yelling obscenities at them in the street.

While May was a guilt-ridden, people-pleasing type of youngster, April was a hellion. She was angry all the time (like her mother, she said) and worried aloud that she might kill someone someday in a fit of rage. She hung out with a tough crowd in the junior high school she attended. With them, she drank alcohol, smoked cigarettes and marijuana, and cut school. She had a hard time keeping friends and had sex with a trail of guys in repetitively misguided attempts to find someone to love and protect her. Invariably, each of these youngsters would mistreat or "go out on" her and each time she reacted with dramatic suffering. Sometimes, she carved their names into her arm with the edge of a paper clip, feeling oddly comforted by the pain she caused herself in the process. Her school grades were barely passing and she seemed not to care. May said April lied all the time, to everyone.

April's attachment to her mother seemed permanently ambivalent. At times, she professed to hate her mother. At other times, she said she cared so little about her mother that she felt guilty. But when her mother seemed to be drinking less, or when April was having trouble at her dad's, then she felt really close to her mother and wanted to be with her. May reported that the relationship was so stormy that she was afraid that their mother would physically hurt April. April, for her part, was afraid that she would physically injure her mother.

Over the course of therapy, which has lasted over five years, April moved back and forth from her father's to her mother's at least a half a dozen times. After about a year of therapy, her father, at the therapist's urging, went to court to get full physical custody and controlled visitation for April. April professed to be furious at him for doing so while blandly accepting that the therapist had written a letter to the court in support of his petition. But her behavior did take its first turn for the better.

At the beginning of treatment, both girls professed affection but not much respect for their father. And both despised their stepmother. She tried too hard, they said, to be the perfect parent. They knew that she had used drugs in her youth and thought her a hypocrite. They complained that she wanted to have meals together "like a family" and that she cooked "health foods," including the dreaded tofu. They complained that she bossed their father around and that she babied her own daughter too much. Nothing she did suited either of them.

April had more trouble at her dad's than May did. She felt like a misfit there, out of place in a controlled and calm environment. She felt like a freak at her dad's. Only at her mom's could she truly be herself.

After about nine months of weekly therapy, April revealed to her sister and then, at May's urging, to the therapist that she had been sexually abused by an older male cousin from the age of six to the age of twelve. This had been her favorite cousin, the only person besides May with whom she had felt truly safe. He had told her that he loved her and would some day marry her. But the sex had been increasingly degrading over time. April had been introduced to fellatio at the age of seven and intercourse at nine. She had been urinated on, rubbed with mud, and made to commit sexual acts with her cousin's friends. Still, she said, she wasn't angry at him like May thought she should be. She thought she even still loved him.

For the next year, April talked about the abuse off and on in therapy. She reported the nightmares she had begun having about her cousin. She talked about feeling dirty and worthless. She began to feel very angry. During this year, her behavior was very stormy. At one point she reported an amnesic episode in which the last thing she remembered was walking by her stepbrother's classroom followed by "awakening" in the nurse's office, having apparently shoved several people along the way.

One day, April reported having been "raped by three guys" over the weekend. She said that she didn't report it because "I hate cops." She seemed completely unruffled in the telling and couldn't offer any details. May privately said that she was certain this hadn't happened. The therapist chose not to directly challenge April's account. Instead, she told April that she was sorry for any suffering that April had endured and hoped that she would become strong enough in time to protect herself and to ask for help when necessary. A couple of months later, April reported having had a "nervous breakdown" at school in which she felt her mind float to the ceiling so that she was watching herself flirting with some guys in the hallway. Over the same months, though, April decreased her drug and alcohol use, seemed less angry overall, and began to adopt a more pro-social identity.

Finally, a year after telling her therapist about the molestation, she told her father and stepmother. Her stepmother immediately believed her, having felt all along that something must account for April's extreme difficulties, and responded with appropriate horror and support. Her father was supportive as well, although in a more subdued way.

Two months later, April showed up at her therapy session with superficial cuts on her thighs. She reported that her cousin, the abuser, had broken into her house in the middle of the night (with her stepmother, father, sister, and stepsister asleep in adjoining rooms) and attacked her. She had told her mother this story and her mother had reported it to the police, who arrested the cousin. April was dismayed. She hadn't thought that her mother would call the police. She was refusing to press charges. Everyone, except possibly April's mother, believed that April had cut herself and made the rest of the story up. Her therapist believed that April wanted to tell her mother, and her mother's side of the family, about the past history of abuse but was afraid that she wouldn't be believed without physical evidence. She told April that it was understandable that someone might do such a thing—tell a lie in order that a more important truth could emerge. April denied that she had done so, but with little anger. In any case, the mission was accomplished: Her mother and grandmother believed her and ostracized the cousin from family events.

Over the next six months, April continued to work on how she felt about herself and how she went about living in the world in light of the sexual abuse. During that time, she also reported getting drunk on alcohol provided by her mother and smoking marijuana with her mother. She talked about a spontaneous miscarriage she had had at age thirteen and about various current relationship issues. Her therapist found it hard to sort out what was true and what was false. She always displayed empathy for April's pain and encouraged her to think of herself as someone who could exert better judgment and control of her life. She encouraged and applauded signs of growth and downplayed or drew lessons from lapses and errors.

At the urging of her therapist, April agreed, at last, to a trial of antidepressant medication. While she didn't stay on the first medicine for very long, a few months later she tried another and found it helpful in containing her rage and keeping her on a more even keel. By this time, she had again left her dad's (after an episode in which he had come home drunk), gone to her mom's where her behavior and mood had deteriorated drastically, and returned to her dad's, after a family meeting in which his sobriety lapse and its meaning for everyone were discussed.

April's recent progress has been heartening. In the last year, she has begun to feel like she "fits" at her dad's. She's even thinking of commuting from home for her first two years of college, since she's not sure she can trust herself to be on her own yet. She has stopped hating her stepmother and even wrote her an unabashedly affectionate Mother's Day card this year. She still sees her mother, partly because she feels attached to her two younger half-siblings, but she no longer expects her mom to stop drinking or get her life together. Her own substance use has declined to a minimal level and her schoolwork has improved. She has developed a passion for art, had a painting exhibited in a regional show, and made honor roll for the first time in her life. She is a bit lonely at present, as she has given up her substance-abusing peer group and not yet replaced them. She also doesn't have a boyfriend at present, but that probably won't last. She's still attracted to dysfunctional guys, whom she hopes she can fix if she loves them enough. While she seems to have some awareness of this pattern, she still perceives each new guy as "really different."

Thinking about the Case

Most clinicians consider borderline personality disorder to be among the most disruptive and costly of all psychiatric conditions. These patients take an inordinate amount of resources: They are seen frequently in hospital emergency rooms for suicidal or self-destructive behavior, and they are often embroiled in the legal system for a variety of reasons including substance abuse, prostitution, and shoplifting, to name just a few. Their difficulties in relationships cause them difficulties in jobs, and they may be high users of public assistance. They tend to "burn out" family and friends so that they come to rely more and more on public systems of care as time goes on.

At the same time, the rage, impulsivity, resistance, and poor insight of these patients make them a therapist's nightmare. They are inclined to miss scheduled appointments but call at 2 A.M. in crisis. They can sit mute for an entire therapy hour or yell obscenities at the therapist. They may be continually suicidal, demanding and rejecting help at every turn. Clinicians typically find themselves uncharacteristically angry and insecure when dealing with individuals with this disorder, and treatment teams find it hard to function harmoniously and consistently in developing plans for care.

Most of the literature on borderline personality disorder focuses on adults; there is little research on the disorder in adolescents and virtually none on preadolescents. The few studies that do exist rely on heterogeneous groups with a variety of co-morbid disorders. Nonetheless, April exhibits many of the following core features of borderline personality disorder: She has a pattern of unstable and intense interpersonal relationships, in particular those with her parents and boyfriends. She has numerous fights, even with her girlfriends. She goes quickly from loving someone to hating that person and back again. Her sister is truly the only person whom she consistently trusts and values. She is markedly impulsive—she uses drugs, has promiscuous sex, cuts school on a moment's notice, and hangs out with the most dangerous elements in her community. She has engaged in self-mutilating behavior, notably cutting herself. She shows marked reactivity of mood, as well. She is frequently angry and irritable and sometimes horribly depressed. Her moods change so frequently and so dramatically that people around her accuse her of faking her feelings and "looking for attention." Her frequent and often inappropriate displays of anger and her difficulty controlling her temper are also characteristic of borderline personality disorder, as are the occasional dissociative episodes she reports, like "blacking out" and feeling as if she is floating outside of her body.

As this case makes clear, borderline personality disorder creates havoc for the sufferer and her family. We say "her" because the disorder is diagnosed much more frequently in girls and women than in boys and men, just as antisocial personality disorder is diagnosed much more often in boys and men than in girls and women. Like all personality disorders, it is apparent by adolescence and generally lasts for several decades, particularly if it is untreated.

The causes of borderline personality disorder are not yet known. Some researchers think that it is a variant of mood disorder, since problems regulating emotion and mood are so prominent in the symptom picture and since some research shows that the disorder runs in the same families in which mood disorders are also found. Others have pointed to the frequency of sexual abuse in the histories of patients with this disorder to suggest that it is really a chronic variant of post-traumatic stress disorder. Still others have suggested that "borderline mothers produce borderline daughters," meaning that a mother's difficulties with empathy and regulation of emotion could hamper her ability to parent a child who is capable of adequately managing painful feelings. As with most of the disorders we discuss, a combination of biological predisposition and precipitating environmental events may be necessary for the development of the actual disorder, with some sufferers showing more of the biological side and others showing more of the environmental side.

The Developmental Perspective

It is rare for a therapist to have the opportunity to follow a patient for five years. This case offers a unique perspective on how psychotherapeutic intervention and normal maturation interact over time. April's therapist paid careful attention to how the normal adolescent issue of developing autonomy was complicated by the disorder. April's ability to separate emotionally from her mother was impaired by their markedly conflictful and abnormally strong bond. The therapist attempted to help April to develop a stable, realistic picture of her mother, so that she herself could develop a stable adjustment to that reality. In addition, April's father and stepmother needed help setting limits on her behavior and following through in the face of her manipulative and sometimes threatening behavior. April desired to make her own decisions, like all adolescents, but her judgment and impulse control were poorly developed. Thus, the process of emerging independence was made more difficult as her parents naturally tried to protect her from making disastrous choices.

This case also highlights the difficulties in diagnosing personality disorders in adolescents. Many of the core features of these disorders—for example, self-centeredness, emotionality, impulsivity, lack of regard for societal rules, odd or eccentric behavior, and problems in relationships—are normative in adolescence. Many adolescents who appear to have personality disorders later "recover" to a well-functioning adulthood.

While the course of personality disorders over time has not been fully clarified by research, it is generally thought that individuals improve somewhat in the fourth and fifth decades of life as the fires that fuel emotions in adolescence and young adulthood naturally die back somewhat. Individuals with borderline personality disorder may be able to attain more stable, albeit not very satisfying, relationships as they age. Generally, their impulsive, self-destructive behavior subsides to some extent as well.

Questions to Consider

1. April and May are very different, despite being raised in the same circumstances. What are some possible reasons that this is so?

2. April's therapy consisted mostly of individual sessions with occasional consultations for her parents. Would you have chosen to work differently? Why or why not?

3. What are some possible explanations for the fact that borderline personality disorder is diagnosed more often in females than in males? Can you suggest an experiment or study that might shed light on which explanation(s) might be correct?

4. Consider the hypothesis that borderline personality disorder is the female equivalent of antisocial personality disorder. Do you see similarities in the symptoms picture? What other data might help you assess the likelihood that this hypothesis is correct?

5. Keeping in mind a developmental perspective, how might childhood sexual abuse result in the range of symptoms that characterize borderline personality disorder?

6. Do you know anyone who shows symptoms of borderline personality disorder? How does interacting with that person make you feel? Do you observe that there are some areas of functioning that seem untouched by the disorder? If so, what are they?

PART SEVEN

Psychoses

—◄O►—

Most of the disorders included in this volume are familiar in some way to the average reader. Everyone has experienced fear, most of us have felt depressed or elated, and we have all seen both behavioral and developmental disorders in those around us. However, some mental disorders involve a severing of the individual's connection with reality so severe that his or her behavior is virtually incomprehensible. These disorders are called "psychoses." Their hallmark symptoms include (1) delusions, which are false ideas that are not correctible by reasoning, (2) hallucinations, which are sensory perceptions in the absence of appropriate stimuli, and (3) ideas of reference, for example, that the radio is sending you a special coded message.

While psychoses can be associated with organic conditions like head injury and substance abuse, we have chosen to include in this section two cases of schizophrenia, which emerges, for reasons that are still mysterious, generally during adolescence and which is among the most disabling of all the mental and emotional disorders. It has been said that "to know schizophrenia is to know psychiatry." This is because schizophrenia contains all of the essential mysteries: How is it that a person can "hear" voices when no one is present? What are the relative roles of nature and nurture in the development of the illness? Why do some people recover fairly well whereas others remain ill for many years? Further, schizophrenia raises profound social problems as well: Is a person who thinks he's protecting the world from an impostor criminally responsible for taking a potshot at the president? Should we incarcerate people because they are ill and might be dangerous?

Should we treat people against their will when they have a disorder that interferes with their ability to understand that they are ill?

We hope that you will consider all of these issues as you are reading the two cases that follow. In the first, a bright and competent young woman develops schizophrenia abruptly during her sophomore year in college. In the second, a teenager who has struggled through most of his childhood develops schizophrenia more gradually. We have combined the "thinking about the case," "developmental perspectives," and "questions to consider" sections for these two cases so that you will be able to compare and contrast them more easily.

25

SCHIZOPHRENIA WITH ACUTE ONSET: THE CASE OF WENDY W

WENDY WAS A tall, willowy twenty-year-old with a sweet, innocent smile. She wore her straight blond hair loose and dressed in long flowing skirts and simple cotton blouses. She was a knockout. She was also smart. She'd been an honor student in high school, photography editor of the yearbook, and the first of her many friends to get into her first-choice college. She was adored by her father, an Episcopal priest, her mother, a schoolteacher, and her two older brothers. However, in her sophomore year of college the trajectory of Wendy's life was suddenly, unexpectedly, and catastrophically derailed by the abrupt onset of a mental breakdown.

Freshman year had seemed to go well enough, although Wendy had seemed uncharacteristically tentative and insecure. Her parents thought this normal enough, given that this was her first time away from home and she had been the protected "baby" of the family. She made friends quickly and enjoyed her classes, although she was shocked by the extent to which drinking, partying, and sex seemed to dominate campus life. In response, Wendy held fast to her own values and trusted relationships. She kept in close touch with her parents and with her boyfriend of three years, who had gone to a different college several hundred miles away. They would send e-mail to each other several times a day and spoke on the phone about twice a week.

The summer after freshman year, Wendy came home to work and play. She and Robert, her boyfriend, acknowledged that it was strange at first to be back together, but they quickly fell into the old routine and had a wonderful time.

However, shortly before Thanksgiving of sophomore year, Robert broke up with Wendy so that he could begin dating on his own campus. He felt that the distance made their relationship too difficult to sustain.

Wendy appeared to handle the breakup surprisingly well. Her friends and family weren't surprised that she seemed a bit subdued and withdrawn; indeed, they had expected to see more overt signs of emotional upset.

Wendy's parents began to be alarmed when, at Christmas vacation, Wendy announced that she had become interested in the teachings of an Indian guru who was visiting the city in which her college was located. Not only had these teachings led her to become a vegetarian, but she was contemplating dropping out of school to live and work in the guru's enclave. Wendy met each of her parents' objections with a smile and some odd hand gestures whose meaning they could only guess at.

Wendy did drop out of school shortly thereafter and moved in with the guru and other disciples. Within weeks of doing so, her parents received a call from the guru's assistant asking them to come and get her. Apparently, Wendy's behavior had become increasingly bizarre. She had taken to wandering around the house gesturing to people and speaking in sentences that didn't make any sense. She seemed to think that the guru understood her, but he did not. She frequently laughed out loud or answered questions that no one had asked. When she took it into her head to "bring the word" to the neighbors, her housemates tried to restrain her. Shockingly, she had turned on them, accusing them of trying to interfere with her divine function, given to her by God and communicated to her through the guru's thoughts. She had picked up a kitchen knife and threatened to slash anybody who tried to stop her.

Wendy's parents assured the woman who called that they would be there as quickly as possible, but when they arrived they found that Wendy had already been taken to a local hospital by the police. While Wendy had been temporarily calmed by intervention from the guru himself, later that night she rose from bed, took off her clothes, and lit some candles, which she carried from room to room, chanting nonsense in the loudest possible voice. Even the guru was unable to settle her down this time, and so the police had been called.

Wendy's parents were horrified by her appearance and behavior at the hospital. She was virtually mute and seemed extremely suspicious of them. She chanted some syllables under her breath the entire time they were there. She seemed to be concentrating on something that they could not apprehend and was unable to carry on even the simplest conversation. She seemed to believe that the hospital was giving her poisoned food and she declared that she would eat nothing while she was there.

Wendy's provisional diagnosis was schizophreniform disorder: a brief, schizophrenia-like psychosis of less than six months' duration. She was treated with medication (for which a court order had to be obtained since she refused to take anything by mouth) and lots of low-key support. Within a week she had resumed eating, and within two weeks the gestures, mumbling, and confusion began to abate. By the time another two weeks had gone by, she seemed much like her old self and was pleading with her parents and her doctor to let her go back to school.

Wendy didn't understand why she had had such strange thoughts and experiences. With embarrassment, she related to her parents that she had believed that the guru was sending her telepathic messages that only she could receive. She had become convinced that she was his female counterpart, half of the "yin and yang," destined to save the world. She had thought her parents and the hospital staff had made a pact with the devil to stop her. She had been confused and frightened, but gradually she had regained her senses. She figured that the stress of school and her breakup with her boyfriend had precipitated her "breakdown," and she wanted nothing except to return to her previous life.

Wendy's doctor recommended that she return to school part time at first and attend a day-treatment program at the hospital as well. He also instructed her to continue taking her medication once she was released. Over his objections, but with her parents' support, Wendy resumed a full academic load. She did agree to see an outpatient therapist once a week, in addition to monthly sessions with her doctor to monitor her progress and manage her medication.

Back at school, Wendy threw herself into her studies. She also plunged into social activities, determined to convince herself and everyone else that she was "normal." Her friends didn't know what to make of the change in her. She seemed anxious and on edge. She began to drink at parties and had a couple of uncharacteristically casual sexual encounters. Her attempts to fit in seemed brittle and forced.

In therapy, Wendy talked about the stigma of mental illness. She revealed how frightened she was of the future, how shaken her confidence in herself had been, how guilty she felt about the suffering she had inflicted on her parents. She was determined to put the trauma totally in the past.

The semester went well, all in all. Wendy's grades were not as high as usual, but she passed everything. That summer, she came home and began working at the law office where she had worked the summer before. Robert was home as well and Wendy found seeing him and talking with him quite painful. He wanted them to be friends, but trying to do so took a quiet toll on her. Without her therapist to talk to, and with a strong need to hide from her friends at home what her semester had really been like, Wendy felt lonely and isolated.

Wendy's psychiatrist had given her a three-month supply of medicine before she left school. As summer wore on, she began to feel that taking it no longer made sense. After all, she had been well for months—no sign of crazy ideas or special messages. In addition, the medicine had increased her appetite and she had put on thirty pounds. Feeling unattractive and embarrassed, she had had to find ways to avoid appearing in a bathing suit. The medicine dulled her concentration and made her sleepy. So, on July 4th, she "liberated" herself from it without telling her parents, who she knew would object.

The rest of the summer actually went better. Wendy lost some weight, felt more clearheaded, and regained some confidence. By fall, she felt more than ready to return to school. She resumed her monthly meetings with the psychiatrist (even though she had secretly stopped taking the pills), but decided she didn't need to see her therapist any more.

However, almost as soon as the semester commenced, Wendy began to feel overwhelmed by the workload. She couldn't seem to concentrate as well as usual and she found it hard to memorize material. She responded by increasing the number of hours she spent on her work, determined to succeed. One day, alone in the library, she became convinced that a paragraph she had just read held special meaning for her. Within the next few days, she was getting coded messages from the radio and television. Again, her behavior became increasingly bizarre, and within ten days a call from her roommate prompted her parents to take steps to have her rehospitalized.

This time, the six-months'-duration criterion for a diagnosis of schizophrenia (rather than the briefer schizophreniform disorder) had been met, making the prognosis more grave. It now seemed clear that Wendy would need to be in treatment for an extended period of time if she were to maintain her high level of functioning.

Again, medication and supportive therapy were effective in helping Wendy regain a footing in reality. However, Wendy's return to the real world was accompanied by marked chagrin and fear for the future. She hadn't been able to make it on her own. What would become of her? Must she give up all of her plans for the future? For the first time, thoughts of killing herself began to flit through Wendy's mind.

Before she was discharged, Wendy and her parents had a meeting with her psychiatrist and therapist. Together they talked about the diagnosis and its implications. Long-term treatment was mandatory. Avoidance of stress would be helpful. Wendy would have to learn about schizophrenia and become committed to her own recovery.

Learning that there were concrete steps that she could take to remain well helped lift Wendy's depression. With the support of her family, friends, and treatment team, and as a result of her own dedication to overcoming the potential pitfalls posed by her illness, Wendy has done well for the past five years. She has not been rehospitalized, although her medication has had to be adjusted from time to time as her symptoms have waxed and waned. She has just earned a bachelor's degree, although it took her an extra year to do so. She is about to begin her first job.

Wendy is careful to get enough rest, to eat properly, and to exercise well. She pushes herself to talk about her illness with selected friends, so that they will understand her need to do what it takes to "keep myself together" and so that they will be able to help her see if she is developing symptoms again. While she knows that further breakdowns cannot be ruled out, Wendy is cautiously hopeful that she will be able to succeed in meeting her life goals. Those who love her are betting on her, too.

[This case is discussed with the next case on schizophrenia on pages 191–194.]

26

SCHIZOPHRENIA WITH INSIDIOUS ONSET: THE CASE OF JESSE P

JESSE HAD ALWAYS been a difficult child. Colicky as an infant, active and willful as a child, he had exhausted his mother, Ruth, and frustrated his father, Tony. As a toddler, he broke his little sister's toys, twisted her arm when he got mad, and couldn't sit still long enough for his mother to read him a story. Needless to say, school became a battleground. Jesse seemed unable (or unwilling—nobody could say for sure) to follow even simple instructions. His temper tantrums landed him in the principal's office several times a week. His speech was delayed and his reading skills were poor.

Tony and Ruth were conscientious parents. Hardworking, second-generation Italian Americans, they wanted the best for their son. They were also deeply embarrassed by his behavior, which they felt to be a reflection on their adequacy as parents. While Tony buried his fears and frustrations in work, Ruth made the rounds of doctors, speech therapists, teachers, and social workers, looking for some key to unlocking Jesse's innate potential. One physician said that Jesse was brain damaged and couldn't be helped. Another said that he was hyperactive and needed medication. The medicine seemed to help a bit, but Tony was adamantly opposed to Jesse's taking it, and after a few weeks Ruth gave in to his wishes. One of the therapists they consulted said that Ruth and Tony needed to exert more discipline, but she never said how they were to do this. School officials said that Jesse was just lazy, that he'd rather act like a clown than apply himself to work.

By fifth or sixth grade, it had become clear that Jesse was losing the struggle, both academically and socially. He had only a few friends, who were generally misfits like himself. Other children avoided him or derided him. Once sensitive and easily hurt, he gradually became tougher and affected an "I don't give a damn" attitude.

At home, he ruled the roost when his father wasn't around. He terrorized both his sister and his mother by pushing them around when they annoyed him. Ruth took to hiding the bruises on her arms, lest Tony see them and fly into a rage at Jesse. She tried to protect Jesse, not only from his father's anger but from the negative judgments of friends and family. She felt that he couldn't help himself most of the time and, feeling guilty and sorry for him, she tried to make up for the lack of affection he received from others. Tony and her own mother said that she spoiled Jesse. Arguments about how to manage his behavior seemed to dominate the household. Meanwhile, Jesse's sister found herself wishing that he'd never been born, even though she, too, felt sorry for him some of the time.

By seventh grade, Jesse had discovered cigarettes, alcohol, and marijuana. Sometimes with friends but often alone, he'd cut school and head for the park to get stoned and listen to rock music on his boom box. Despite his parents' exhortations, bribes, and diatribes, he failed seventh grade, repeated it successfully, passed eighth by the skin of his teeth, and then failed ninth.

With increasing drug use, Jesse's behavior got more and more erratic. Once he threw a pitchfork at his father and then ran away to a neighboring city. His father pressed charges for assault so that Jesse could be placed on probation for a time, but his behavior didn't really change. By high school, he was almost entirely isolated from social contacts. At home, he spent virtually all of his time alone in his room, listening to rock music at ear-shattering volume. He spent hours in the shower each day and insisted that his meals be brought to him. He became interested in the occult, began to talk more and more about the devil, and then, one day, accused his mother of being a witch. Finally, just before his sixteenth birthday, Jesse completely lost contact with reality.

On a Saturday alone with his father, he became frightened that his father had become infected with evil spirits. Frantically, he insisted that his father shower at once and, completely nonplussed, Tony agreed. He emerged from the shower just in time to see Jesse, stark naked, burying something in the backyard. Before Tony could decide what to do, Jesse came back in and ordered his father to remove his wedding band and get back into the shower. The rock in Jesse's hand and the wild look in his eye convinced Tony to comply. When Jesse ran back outside, Tony called the police and Jesse was taken to the emergency room of the local hospital, where he was committed for observation and treatment.

In the hospital, Jesse was fearful and withdrawn. The nurses observed that he sometimes shouted or laughed inappropriately, apparently in response to voices only he could hear. Twice he had to be forcibly isolated after menacing another patient, who, he insisted, had been putting "bad thoughts" into his mind. After a month of taking medicine and attending various therapy sessions, Jesse was improved enough to go home. Sadly, this was not the end of Jesse's struggle.

Jesse spent a total of about three of the next eight years hospitalized, although each hospitalization lasted no more than a few months. By the third hospitalization, the diagnosis of schizophrenia, paranoid type, had been firmly established. Each time he was treated with medication, which helped him regain a firmer hold on reality. He also had group therapy and individual therapy, designed to help him learn about his illness, set goals for himself, and develop some social skills.

Jesse's condition improved noticeably during each hospitalization, but despite repeatedly promising at the end of each inpatient stay that he would attend outpatient therapy programs, he never followed through. Instead, he returned home where he slept most of the day and wandered about most of the night, smoking cigarettes and listening to music. Invariably, he would discard his medication and return to a pattern of alcohol and marijuana use. Just as invariably, within a few weeks of renewed substance abuse he would begin hearing voices and become convinced others could control his thoughts. Always his bizarre, irrational behavior would cause him to be rehospitalized.

Finally, exhausted and at wits' end, Tony and Ruth accepted the advice that hospital social workers had given them from the beginning: They refused to let Jesse come home and, instead, made arrangements for him to be discharged to a group home where twelve adults with mental illness lived together in a house, supervised by a staff of resident counselors. Over the next decade, the frequency and length of his hospitalizations gradually decreased. With numerous steps backward, he gradually progressed from the group home to a supervised apartment setting. He spent his days in various educational or work training settings, most of which he dropped out of after a while and to some of which he returned more than once.

Jesse is now thirty-eight years old. While he has not been hospitalized in two years, he lives his life at the margins of society. He has a small apartment, paid for by social security disability payments. He attends a prevocational program sporadically. He also attends a "dual-diagnosis" support group for people with mental illness who also have substance abuse problems. He has made a few friends along the way, people with mental health problems like himself. Most of his socializing, though, is done with his parents, whom he visits several times a week. He showers, does his laundry, and eats his only hot meals at their house.

Jesse's hostility seems virtually gone but so do his energy and zest for life. He doesn't talk as much about witches and devils, although he still believes in them, but he and his dad can talk about football and baseball together. He takes his medication more or less regularly, although he complains from time to time that it makes him feel heavy, "fuzzy," and slow. He smokes marijuana only rarely and seems to have given up alcohol completely, although he still smokes cigarettes. His parents have lowered their expectations. They no longer hope for a "cure," through which Jesse will get a job, a wife, a "normal" life. Now they hope for a modicum of stability and dignity for him—and they wonder who will care for him when they are gone.

Thinking about the Cases

Approximately one out of every hundred people will be diagnosed with schizophrenia at some time in their lives. The peak age of onset for this often chronic, debilitating illness is late adolescence through young adulthood. It is diagnosed rarely in youngsters under fifteen or in adults over thirty. The symptoms of schizophrenia are so vivid that few observers would dispute that the person is ill. The "positive symptoms" include delusions (false beliefs that are not correctible by reasoning), hallucinations (sensory experiences in the absence of appropriate stimuli), and disorganized speech or behavior. Some people also experience what are called "negative symptoms." These include an apparent narrowing of the emotional range, inability to experience pleasure, decreased motivation, lack of attention to self-care, and social withdrawal. While both Jesse and Wendy experienced all three of the positive symptoms, only Jesse showed prominent negative symptoms.

Schizophrenia is only one of several disorders in which psychosis is the defining symptom. A psychotic episode or state is a period of time in which a person has lost contact with reality. A psychotic illness or psychosis is one in which the person experiences psychotic episodes. Individuals with schizophrenia are not always psychotic: Wendy, for example, had long periods of normalcy interspersed with relatively brief psychotic episodes. Nor are all individuals with psychosis necessarily schizophrenic: Some have brief psychotic episodes or episodes related to drug use, for example.

Schizophrenia is a multidimensional disorder. While research indicates that individuals with schizophrenia have disordered brain bio-chemistry, and possibly even anatomical differences, the timing and severity of episodes are affected by environmental stressors. Further, some sufferers have a family history of schizophrenia or related disorders, leading to the hypothesis that genetics plays a role in the etiology of the illness in at least a subset of sufferers. While early studies examining the role of parental behavior in the development of schizophrenia have not led to fruitful conclusions, the role of the family as one of several nonspecific stressors (or protectors) cannot be ruled out.

In any case, how the individual will fare in the long run depends on the adequacy of treatment, the skills and strengths that the individual brings to the table, the nature and extent of the social support system, and the presence or absence of associated disorders like substance abuse and depression. In general, people like Wendy who have a history of success before the first episode, who do not have preexisting or associated psychological disorders or substance abuse, and who experience primarily positive symptoms with acute onset are thought to have a better prognosis than those like Jesse, who has an illness that worsens gradually, a history of inadequate functioning, concurrent substance abuse, and prominent negative symptoms between episodes of acute psychosis. How the individual handles social stigma, disappointment, and frustration will also affect the prognosis, as will his capacity for insight and ability to cooperate with treatment.

Since schizophrenia is multidimensional, so is its treatment. The cornerstone, for virtually all patients, is medication. There are currently over two dozen medicines used to treat schizophrenia, with many more in the research pipeline. They work to rebalance the neurotransmitters in the brain, particularly the neurotransmitter dopamine, which seems to be particularly implicated in schziophrenia. For most patients, the medications work imperfectly, leaving some residual symptoms, causing annoying (and occasionally dangerous) side effects, and requiring long-term (possibly lifelong) use. However, many patients stop taking their medication at some point in the recovery process, and the majority of these have a relapse.

Hospitalization is often used to restabilize a person and provide protection from both danger and stress when a relapse has occurred. While in the past individuals with schizophrenia would spend the majority of their lives in large, impersonal psychiatric institutions, today most are treated for a few weeks at a time in small psychiatric units of general hospitals and then discharged to semistructured environments like a halfway house or a day-treatment program.

To guard against relapse, education about the chronic nature of schizophrenia and the various aspects of the treatment plan is generally provided to both the patient and involved family members. In addition, psychotherapy can be helpful—not in curing the illness, but in helping the individual cope with it most successfully. Group therapy and family therapy also have their place with some patients.

In addition to treatment of the illness itself, most sufferers require some rehabilitation efforts as well since cognitive and social deficits may remain even after acute symptoms have receded. Specialized education programs, training or retraining in skills related to living independently and working, and sheltered or supervised work situations are among the methods commonly used.

Wendy and Jesse represent two different points on the continuum of outcome in schizophrenia. For some people, the illness is lifelong and severely debilitating. For others, symptoms are manageable and interfere minimally with life goals. For most, an outcome somewhere in the middle is likely. Recovery is slow, marked by setbacks and dependent on some revision of life plans. Recent studies indicate that while short- and intermediate-term outcomes are frequently disappointing, long-term outcome (twenty years or more after onset of illness) is actually fairly good, with the majority of people living in the community with a satisfactory quality of life and few disturbing symptoms.

The Developmental Perspective

Schizophrenia's impact on development is frequently profound, coming as it does during adolescence when a great deal of learning and changing occurs. Since recovering some stability can take several years after the onset of the disorder, many patients describe having lost their dating years to the illness. One young man found himself at age twenty-six a sophomore in college after having spent seven years in and out of hospitals and halfway houses. He felt he had the emotional and dating skills of an adolescent but was expected to behave as an adult. A virgin, insecure, and self-stigmatized, he felt totally incompetent. Vocational skills and interests are often honed during this period as well, as is the development of a stable self-image—these, too, can be derailed by schizophrenia.

In addition, adolescence is the time that young people develop skills for independent living. When their skills are disrupted by an illness like schizophrenia, the normal conflicts of adolescence can be exacerbated. The young person may accuse the parents of being overprotective (a common complaint among normal youngsters) and, because ability is, in fact, compromised by the illness, parents are more protective than they would otherwise be. Often young people with schizophrenia blame their deficits on their parents—"The reason I don't succeed is because you won't let me,"—rather than recognizing the limitations the illness places on their ability to accomplish developmental tasks. Sometimes the illness locks parents and youngsters in dysfunctional patterns of conflict-filled dependency that persist even after symptoms have receded.

The two cases presented above illustrate well how strongly the quality of development before the onset of the illness affects the outcome. Jesse had learned few social abilities and had developed no inner confidence to rely on in his battle with schizophrenia, whereas Wendy had many social and psychological strengths. In general, the more developmental tasks the individual has accomplished and the more adequate their completion has been, the better the prognosis for schizophrenia (and, indeed, for any other psychological disorder).

Finally, schizophrenia is a developmental illness. Why, if it has a strong genetic, biochemical basis, does it wait to show itself until mid to late adolescence? Does puberty function as a biological trigger? Perhaps the social demands of growing up, leaving home, and becoming independent are necessary environmental stressors. Answers to these questions will have to await further research.

Questions to Consider

1. Can you compare and contrast the cases of Jesse and Wendy from a biopsychosocial framework? What is the relative weighting of biological, psychological, and social factors in each case? How are each of these factors related to prognosis?

2. Individuals with schizophrenia who return to family environments in which there is a high rate of criticism and hostility tend to relapse more often than those who return to environments in which these behaviors are less in evidence. What do you make of this? Does it imply anything about the causes of schizophrenia? Why or why not? Would you expect the same finding with other disorders, for example, depression?

3. Other psychological disorders frequently emerge in response or

reaction to the existence of schizophrenia. Can you speculate on which disorders might co-occur with some frequency?

4. Imagine yourself returning to college after having had a "nervous breakdown" that kept you out of school for a semester or two. How would you feel going back? What would you tell your friends? How do you think you would do? Why?

DATE DUE

12-30-01			
5-12-02			
DEC 1 2 2002			
APR 2 0 2004			
7-17-13			
2-23-14			